WHY ME?

FINDING HOPE WHEN LIFE HURTS

RYAN PACK

Auxano
PRESS

Tigerville, South Carolina
www.AuxanoPress.com

ISBN 978-0-578-09237-9

Published by Auxano Press
Tigerville, South Carolina
www.AuxanoPress.com

To order additional copies, contact Auxano Press, P.O. Box 315, Tigerville, SC
29688; or order online to www.auxanopress.com.

I dedicate this book to family:

To my wife, Heather, and our four children,
Bailey, Ginny, Victoria, and Micah.
It is an honor to share ministry together.

To my extended family for their support.

To the church families I have had the privilege to serve.
A special thanks to First Baptist Church
of Hendersonville, North Carolina,
for your receptivity to the messages on Job.

Contents

Acknowledgements

I love being a pastor! It is such a joy to watch God transform lives. I have the privilege of delivering the living and active Word of God and watching it change souls.

The recent sermon series I preached on the book of Job had an extraordinary impact on our congregation. In all honesty, I underestimated the impact of Job! The ancient text of Job has life-altering application to our modern day society. Job hurt and wondered what God was doing. Many people in our society today wrestle with the same struggles.

I am so grateful to my church for their hunger for God's Word. They regularly encourage me to preach the Word! This book flows from the sermons that touched their lives.

This project wouldn't be complete without the encouragement from my wife, Heather. She was called to be a pastor's wife and serves in her calling with excellence. I am blessed to have a wife who wants to see God's kingdom expanded at all costs!

I want to thank Ken Hemphill for the opportunity to publish this book. Ken's passion to see the church thrive and his desire to spread the gospel is inspirational. Thank you, Ken and Paula, for your encouragement. It's a joy to be your pastor.

Additional appreciation goes to the staff of First Baptist Church for allowing me the time to complete this book. Thanks for all your hard work. I am truly blessed.

May God's message through the book of Job bring hope to your deepest hurts!

Introduction

It's such a small word. It's only three letters. It's the word "why." But that short little word has many people hung up in terms of their relationship with God. Have you ever felt like you have hit a roadblock or that you are at an absolute standstill in terms of knowing God at a deeper level? You have so many questions that revolve around the word "why." Are you paralyzed right now due to unanswered questions?

As if the word "why" is not difficult enough by itself, it becomes even more personal and painful when the question "why" turns into "why me?" As long as "why" keeps its distance from our lives we can manage or ignore the difficult questions of life. But when "why" intrudes in our personal space then "why me" becomes an unavoidable reality. Regardless of our position in life or stage of life, everyone eventually comes eye-to-eye with the question "why me?"

If our thoughts are reasonable, we understand the reality that life will be difficult at times. We would all agree that life comes with its share of ups and downs. *But here's the really sticky issue: when our life circumstances seem unfair.* Difficulties in life we can accept; unfairness causes us to wrestle. It is the injustice that causes us to shake our fist at God. When the activity descending from heaven seems wrong, we sometimes respond with anger and frustration. You know the questions you have asked… "Why now? Why this situation? Why this timing? Why this reoccurrence? Why this pain? Why me?"

God knew we would have questions and wrestle with pain,

1

so He has provided for us, in the pages of His holy scriptures, the book of Job, answers for such questions. Job endured unbelievable pain but held on to God with unshakable faith. When we discover the details concerning the greatness of Job, it places the questions concerning unfair and unjust circumstances in even greater perspective.

The book of Job is 42 chapters. It is one of the longer books in the Bible. You have to fasten your seatbelt because we are covering 42 chapters in this brief book. The reason that we can do this is because Job is really a simple book in its structure. It can be outlined like this: Part 1—Job is tested (chapters 1-2). Part 2—Lengthy dialogue between Job and his friends (chapters 4-37). Job's friends are determined to set him straight by attempting to figure out, in their own wisdom, why Job faces such great pain. Isn't it interesting that the bulk of the book of Job is dedicated to human attempts to explain why God does what He does? Yet God answers Job in only four chapters. This is a reminder that we often spend way too much time trying to deduce the ways of God rather than spending sufficient time simply listening to God. Part 3—God answers (chapters 38-41). After the friends give their human solutions to this age old question to suffering, we get to the really good part when God answers. Part 4—Job is completely restored (chapter 42).

Here it is in a nutshell: Job is tested. The friends try to figure out his pain. God answers and Job is restored. So there are only four major outline points to all 42 chapters of this intriguing book of the Bible.

I love what Eugene Peterson writes about the book of Job.

> It is not only because Job suffered that he is important to us. It is because he suffered in the same ways that we suffer – in the vital areas of family, personal health, and material things. Job is also

important to us because he searchingly questioned and boldly protested his suffering. Indeed, he went "to the top" with his questions.

It is not the suffering that troubles us. It is undeserved suffering. Almost all of us in our years of growing up have the experience of disobeying our parents and getting punished for it. When that discipline was connected with wrongdoing, it had a certain sense of justice to it: When we do wrong, we get punished.

One of the surprises as we get older, however, is that we come to see that there is no real correlation between the amount of wrong we commit and the amount of pain we experience. An even larger surprise is that very often there is something quite the opposite: We do right and get knocked down. We do the best we are capable of doing, and just as we are reaching out to receive our reward we are hit from the blind side and sent reeling.[1]

I have to be very open with you and acknowledge that this wasn't an easy book to write. This isn't one of those topics that gives you a warm fuzzy feeling. This isn't one of those talks where we walk away with cotton candy and lollipops and act like everything is just fine and dandy. This is one of those books of the Bible that goes to the core. It requires us to wrestle with the reality of life. It's where the rubber meets the road.

Throughout this book we are going to wrestle with loss of money and possessions. We are going to grapple with the specter of death. We are going to struggle with issues related to physical illness. This book forces us to take a close look at many of the deep pains that are visiting our lives and the lives of our family and friends right now.

I must tell you from the very beginning that although this book is titled *Why Me*, we will not be able to answer every question in life. As finite humans with limited understanding we will never completely understand the unlimited and eternal nature of Almighty God.

But we are going to do our best to discover how Job handled difficulties and learn from some of his breakthroughs and victories. We are also going to learn from the moments when Job wants to shake his fist at God. Most importantly, we are going to learn more about the nature and activity of Almighty God. After all, isn't knowing God more intimately the ultimate goal in all seasons of life? And yes, even the painful seasons can help us to learn more about God.

---

1   Eugene H. Peterson, "Introduction to Job," from The Message (Colorado Springs, CO: NavPress, 2002) 839.

CHAPTER ONE

Meet the Man

Before we can set sail into this journey designed to help us understand "why me," we must first have a solid understanding of the man Job. Knowing more about Job brings us in touch with the personal side of his pain. He is a real man facing real pain. Let's take a look at Job 1:1-5.

> In the land of Uz there lived a man whose name was Job. This man was blameless and upright; he feared God and shunned evil. He had seven sons and three daughters, and he owned seven thousand sheep, three thousand camels, five hundred yoke of oxen and five hundred donkeys, and had a large number of servants. He was the greatest man among all the people of the East. His sons used to take turns holding feasts in their homes, and they would invite their three sisters to eat and drink with them. When a period of feasting had run its course, Job would send and have them purified. Early in the morning he would sacrifice a burnt offering for each of them, thinking, "Perhaps my children have sinned and cursed God in their hearts." This was Job's regular custom.

The first five verses of chapter 1 give us a wealth of detail about Job. First of all, we see he was a good man. It says very clearly in the scripture that he was blameless and upright. The scripture even goes as far as calling Job "the greatest man in the

East." So he was a very, very *good man*.

A second detail that takes his life to another level is that he was a *godly man*. It is one thing to say that someone is an honest, upright, moral person. Those are great qualities and characteristics, but the scripture goes beyond this description and indicates that he feared God and he shunned evil. He was such a godly man he didn't want a hint of evil in his family. When his children celebrated feasts, he wanted to make sure that they did not sin in their hearts. He sacrificed burnt offerings and interceded on behalf of his family. This attribute leads us to the third quality of Job.

He was a *praying man*. It is important to notice that verse 5 indicates that when the period of feasting had run its course Job would send for his children and have them purified. Early in the morning he would sacrifice a burnt offering for each of his children. He had seven sons and three daughters; every day he interceded on behalf of each of his ten children. The Bible tells us that prayers and intercession were Job's regular custom.

The fourth quality of Job is that he was a *wealthy man*. The record of Job's wealth may not mean much to you in the twenty-first century, but it speaks volumes in an ancient culture. The Bible says he has 7,000 sheep, 3,000 camels, 500 yoke of oxen, 500 donkeys, and a large number of servants. Your first impression may be "So what? Job had a large number of animals and servants." The specifics given here are intended to open our eyes to the magnitude of his wealth.

Basically the scripture has just shown us Job's balance sheet. We have been allowed to get an insider's view of his portfolio. Anyone in this day who had 3,000 camels would have basically owned UPS and FedEx put together. The camels were the shipping industry. Some commentators call him the Steve Jobs, Warren Buffet and Bill Gates of the day. He was just an extremely wealthy man. His reputation as a wealthy and upright man was known throughout the East.

Lastly, what we know about him is that he was a *family man*. We know he was a good man, a godly man, a praying man, and a wealthy man, but now we discover that he was also a family man. At this stage in his life, Job's children are grown and have established families of their own. Yet Job is still interceding for his children one by one. So he is a family man.

Why does the Bible give us such a detailed description of this man? Why have I taken the time to relate all of this detail? If we are to fully appreciate the events to come in Job's life, we must get to know Job intimately. God wanted us to understand that being a good man (or woman) or a godly man or a praying man, or a wealthy man, or a family man does not make Job immune from the challenges of life.

There lived a man

"In the land of Uz there lived a man" (1:1). Before we get to all the descriptors that tell us that Job was a good man, a godly man, a praying man, a wealthy man and a family man, we are told simply about "a man." The adjectives that later describe Job give us great detail about the man, but first and foremost we are introduced to "a man." Job was a human being just like each one of us. We all have this in common.

This truth sets the stage for the rest of the story. When we watch someone go through pain, the first thing we do is go through a list of qualifiers about the person. For example we may say, "Bless their heart, (that's how we start conversations in the south), I don't know how they can be facing such difficult circumstances. They are such a good person. How can God allow such difficult circumstances to enter the life of such an upright citizen of our community? They go to church. They give money. They give their time. They are spiritual or God fearing." The list of noteworthy qualities could go on and on. But first and foremost the Bible says that in the land of Uz there lived a man.

Why am I dwelling on this simple descriptor? It is critical that we first understand who we are. Before we can discuss good and evil and before we can understand the will of God, we must start with a very clear realization of our position and, most importantly, God's position. Our position is that we are man or woman, created by God. *We are man, not God!*

Now here's the trap that many of us fall into—a trap which causes us to wrestle with the inequities of life. We think we are Superman or Wonder Woman. In other words, we believe we should be invincible to whatever comes our way. We shouldn't feel or experience the pain of "mere mortals." Some of you may have recently said or thought, "I shouldn't have any of this pain and discomfort in my life because I am an upright, moral, good, godly person." Feel free to add any other descriptor which comes to mind. But the bottom line is that we are all human, we are flesh and blood.

When we go through struggles we are first tempted to elevate ourselves to the status of God. We find ourselves saying, "God, this is not fair. This is not the way I would have done it. This suffering doesn't fit my schedule. This doesn't fit my plan and this is not how I would have put the pieces together." When we do this, we move from being "just" man to playing God. It's as if we forget that we are human and God is God. The book of Job sets the record straight right out of the starting gate—"In the land of Uz there lived a *man*." (emphasis mine)

Here's a simple exercise that may free you up to cope with the circumstances you are facing. Say this with me—"I am not

Superman." Maybe God is trying to teach us to take the "S" off of our chest and put it back in its rightful place...at the throne of God. When we ask the question, "Why me?," we are subtly implying that an all-wise and all-merciful God has made a mistake. Why not ask the question—"Why not me?" Do you know who you are? Do you know what you are? Just men and women—just human. So let's say it together... I am not a superhero. I am not invincible. I am not God.

The first five verses of chapter 1 have set a critical foundation for the rest of the book of Job. We are now acquainted with Job, a man with many admirable qualities. Qualities that we assume would make him somehow exempt from trouble. Wouldn't a man who God Himself calls "my servant" get a free pass from the dark side of life? Don't overlook the fact that the Bible records in Job 1:8 that God said: "There is no one on earth like him; he is blameless and upright, a man who fears God and shuns evil."

Before we move to the next chapter, would you be willing to put aside all of the great adjectives about yourself that you think should exempt you from pain? Would you admit to God right now that you are just a man or a woman surrendered to His sovereign will over your preset agenda? If we are going to successfully wrestle with the deep issues of "why," we must ask ourselves, how do I view myself? Do I think I deserve certain "perks" in the Christian faith because of my goodness? We cannot understand more about God when we are too full of ourselves.

CHAPTER TWO

Behind the Scenes

Let's continue on our journey through the book of Job. In the first five verses, we were provided with a detailed description of the man. But now the scene changes dramatically. There is an interlude almost like a commercial break during a television broadcast. But during our interlude, we are transported into a whole new realm. We are allowed to look at a scene that occurs in the heavenlies, a conversation between God and Satan, a conversation about which Job has no knowledge.

This heavenly conversation is taking place while Job is happily living life as a godly, wealthy, God-fearing, family man of impeccable integrity. He has no clue of the trouble headed his way. While we are given a more complete picture of coming events, Job doesn't enjoy the luxury of seeing into the other world. He didn't know that God and the accuser were talking; therefore, Job had no idea what was about to happen.

Here is a fundamental truth we must accept as we continue to address the question "why." There is a world beyond this world. There are events happening right now in the spiritual realm that are beyond our ability to see and understand. The sovereign Almighty God is at work. At the same moment an enemy, ready to destroy God's good work, is active in ways we can't see. There is a spiritual battle between good and evil. While the adversary is working to steal, kill, and destroy, God is providing protection based on His immutable character and principles.

What happens in the unseen world is often the groundwork

for that which is experienced in our lives as the unexpected challenge. We can't see the battle, but the results make an appearance in our life in something known as the "unexpected." We can all relate to…the unexpected. It may be the dreaded doctor's appointment when the test results are to be returned. It may come in the form of the late night call from the highway patrol informing us of the accident. It may be as a nondescript envelope sent from corporate headquarters with the pink slip enclosed. It always catches us off-guard. The "unexpected" is the unseen revealed.

We don't schedule pain. We don't place a traffic accident on our calendar for this Thursday at 5:00. We don't scratch on our monthly to-do list "broken marriage toward the end of the month." It just shows up—uninvited but clearly announced. The unseen makes its grand entrance into our lives. Since we don't get to schedule "the unexpected" it comes with great surprise. The unseen becomes seen. And we start asking "Why Me?" To make any progress, we must realize that events do happen behind the scenes that are beyond our knowledge, sight and understanding. Yet they impact our daily lives.

So how do we live today in our world when events are happening in an unseen world that are out of our hands and out of our control? Let me bring it down to earth with the simplicity of a 4 x 6 picture. During a recent worship service at First Baptist Hendersonville, I showed a picture from a beach vacation. It was a picture of my family with some of our extended family in front of the beautiful inlet waters of the South Carolina coast. The sky was a vivid blue with no clouds in sight. The water was calm. The vegetation in the marsh glistened with multiple hues of green. All looked beautiful. All seemed picturesque.

Although the view in the snapshot looked perfect you must

understand that the view from that 4 x 6 was limited. When you look at a snapshot all you see is that frame. You cannot see beyond the borders of that picture. I had an advantage since I was there at the moment in time when the picture was taken. I saw beyond the frame. Remember I told you that at the moment of the picture, the water was calm and all looked perfect. But beyond that frame there was a world of chaos. Boats passed through the waters every minute. Jet skis zoomed by leaving their wake in the water. To the left of the snapshot were crowds of people sitting in lawn chairs. To the right were more vacationers and barking dogs. In front of my family were dozens of cars in a parking area. You see, if you aren't there in the moment, you are limited to a single frame.

This is life. We have to live it one frame at a time. Some of you have gone through darkness and valleys that I can't wrap my mind around. Some of you have faced tragedy, sickness, loss, and unfathomable pain. Yet even in the pain all we get is one frame of the picture. One snapshot. While we are living with the reality of one frame at a time, we must remember that God sees the whole picture. The boats, the noisy people, the barking dogs, the speeding jet skis and beyond. He knows what is going on above us, below us, around us, and on each side of us. He is the Alpha and Omega. He is the beginning and the end. He is unlimited. He is not bound by time or location. His view takes in the scope of our entire life while we can only see one small frame.

We must see each day as a new frame. Remember that His mercies are new every morning. Lamentations 3:22-23 states, "Because of the LORD's great love we are not consumed, for his compassions never fail. They are new every morning; great is your faithfulness." Every morning we get a new frame that lasts 24 hours. Each month we get another four weeks of new frames. We know what is in our present frame, but guess what? We have no clue what the next frame will hold.

Let's make sure we understand this…I am clueless about the next frame of my life. Join the human race, all of us are clueless concerning what's going on outside our small frame. We are inexperienced concerning what might show up in the next frame. None of us know what is happening behind the scenes that will suddenly show up in our frame.

Armed with this knowledge about the unseen, let's revisit the dialogue between God and Satan. Remember this conversation is happening in another realm completely out of Job's view. Here's how the Bible records the event.

> One day the angels came to present themselves before the LORD, and Satan also came with them. The LORD said to Satan, "Where have you come from?" Satan answered the LORD, "From roaming through the earth and going back and forth in it." Then the LORD said to Satan, "Have you considered my servant Job? There is no one on earth like him; he is blameless and upright, a man who fears God and shuns evil." "Does Job fear God for nothing?" Satan replied. "Have you not put a hedge around him and his household and everything he has? You have blessed the work of his hands, so that his flocks and herds are spread throughout the land. But stretch out your hand and strike everything he has, and he will surely curse you to your face." The LORD said to Satan, "Very well, then, everything he has is in your hands, but on the man himself do not lay a finger." Then Satan went out from the presence of the LORD. (Job 1:6-12)

To understand this passage we need to have a clear understanding of the Hebrew word for "Satan." In the original language the word "Satan" literally means "accuser." If you have ever wondered why Satan is called the accuser, it is simply because Satan is the one who makes accusations. He is one who accuses men, not to bring them to repentance but to tempt them to fail. Hold on to this understanding of Satan's name because it will bring greater depth to our study in just a moment.

Here's the dialogue in a summary fashion. The accuser says to God that Job only trusts you and only follows you and only loves you because of the blessings you have given him. Remember what the passage says: "You have blessed the work of his hands, so that his flocks and herds are spread throughout the land. But stretch out your hand and strike everything he has, and he will surely curse you to your face" (1:10). So the accuser argues that Job is righteous because it pays. Therefore, he suggests that if God removes all of Job's possessions then Job will curse the very name of God.

Don't forget that we have already had a glimpse at Job's bulging portfolio. Job is blessed financially. He is blessed with a large family. He is well-known throughout the entire region. Job has it all! Not only do we know that Job is richly blessed, but the accuser is also aware of Job's stuff and his status. Satan is basically saying to God, "Check Job's motives. Does Job love you because of the stuff or does he love you because you are God? Does he love you because of what you give him or does he love you because of who you are?"

I cannot, on this side of heaven, answer every question about every struggle and every pain in every circumstance in every dark valley. None of us can. I am convinced, based on the pages of scripture, that God tests us and allows the accuser to make accusations about us to find out our true motive. Do I love

God for what He gives or do I love God for who He is? That is a question of motive and it is a fundamental question of life. If we are following God for the blessings, we are more liable to question Him or desert Him, when the unseen and unexpected appears to remove the blessings.

So the bottom line gets down to this issue of motive. Would Job still love God, would Job still be blameless? Would he still go to God in prayer if it was all taken away? Would Job still trust God if all the cattle and camels were taken away and his profitable shipping business was shut down? And to make matters even more raw and personal, what would Job do if his kids were taken away? If everything was gone, what would Job do? Can we and will we trust God when we lose our job and adversity seems to be in the only picture frame we can presently see?

I have found in my life, and I see repeated in scripture, that God will often use testing in our lives to surface our motives. There are a lot of things I thought I was supposed to have in life. There are seasons or stages of life I thought I should be allowed to enter. There are events I thought should be on my calendar. But you know what I have found in life—many of those personal desires had nothing to do with God's will. God uses times of pain and difficulty to check our motives.

We humans have a bit of a stubborn streak. Very often that stubbornness will assert: "God, I desire and deserve (just fill in the blank)." Because God is more concerned about our character than our comfort, He will check our motives. It's as if God is saying. "You know what I really need for you to look at is your motive. I am interested in your heart."

Another way to investigate this issue of motive is to ask, "Do we trust God and love Him for who He is or only for the handouts? Do we love Him for *reward* or *relationship*?" Those two words, reward or relationship, really sum up the accusations of the accuser. Satan is saying to God, "This Job guy only loves you for the reward. He loves you because of all the stuff he's accumulated. He's known as the greatest man in the East. You take away the reward, the position and the possessions and let's see if Job still loves you."

Please note the motives of one of God's choicest servants are being tested. God Himself declared, "There is no one on earth like him; he is blameless and upright, a man who fears God and shuns evil" (1:8). Job must have really had his act together for God to say that there was no one else on earth like him. Regardless of our position, status, and list of good works, God will check our motives.

I would even like to propose to you that it is an honor to have God check your motives. Before you put this book down and begin to mumble that I have lost my mind, please hear me out. The scripture tells us that Job is an upright, godly man. We studied the admirable list of Job's characteristics in the first chapter of this book. We know that God speaks of Job with glowing remarks. Yet his motives were tested. Yes, Job knew God well, but God wanted Job to know Him even better. God wanted to make sure all wrong motives were removed from Job's life so there would be room only for God.

Will you trust God enough to let Him check your motives? Would you be willing to take a close look at your heart of hearts? Could it be that we have been serving God because we like the rewards more than the relationship?

A man by the name of Tim Hansel recorded an encounter he had with his son. Many of you parents will be able to relate to circumstances similar to this one.

> One day, while my son Zac and I were out in the country, climbing around in some cliffs, I heard a voice from above me yell, "Hey Dad! Catch me!"

I turned around to see Zac joyfully jumping off a rock straight at me. He had jumped and then yelled "Hey Dad!" I became an instant circus act, catching him. We both fell to the ground. For a moment after I caught him I could hardly talk. When I found my voice again I gasped in exasperation: "Zac! Can you give me one good reason why you did that???" He responded with remarkable calmness: "Sure...because you're my Dad." [1]

We discover in this story that the child's whole assurance was based in the fact that his father was trustworthy. He could live life to the fullest because his father could be trusted. Isn't this even truer for a Christian? How do we jump out in life free floating, wondering what the next frame is going to be? How can we live with such confidence? Because God is our heavenly Father. I don't always understand His ways but I always trust His hand.

---

1   Tim Hansel, *Holy Sweat* (Waco, TX: Word Books Publisher, 1987), 46-47.

CHAPTER THREE

Out of Nowhere

We often use the phrase, "Life is full of surprises." When you think about it, that statement could go in two different directions. You could say, "Yes, life is full of surprises, and I've had some great ones recently." The birth of a child. The joy of new grandchildren. A job promotion. Getting a diamond ring from your high school sweetheart. A bonus check. Life can surely be filled with nice surprises.

But on the other side, when we talk about life being full of surprises many of us have had instances such as a call from our doctor with an unfortunate test result. The surprise could be the drunk driver who ran you off the road. For the dedicated salesman, discouragement sinks in when the big client signs with the other company. We have surprises we like and others we would rather avoid.

We look at the surprise in Job's life. Out of nowhere he encounters a surprise like no other. Job doesn't experience just one bombshell. His come in bundles. No warning! No early signs! No announcement of coming attractions! Seemingly from nowhere comes surprise heaped upon surprise.

I can't tell you how many times I've heard people use the phrase, "out of nowhere" as they share their testimony. Life is sailing along as normal. Everything is in its place. You may even feel as if you are on top of the world. And then you are blindsided. Out of "nowhere" you are hit with pain. Your peace becomes turmoil. The unexpected becomes the new normal.

We love to hear "rags to riches" stories but in the book of

Job we read of a "riches to rags" story. As we study the first test in Job's life, we discover that everything financially is taken from him. His source of income is destroyed. His own wife suggests that Job curse God and die. His friends start to point fingers and dump guilt on his broken soul. Then, as the pain intensifies, the unimaginable occurs. In the last part of this first test, we learn that all ten of his children are taken away from him. Seven sons and three daughters all die in a natural disaster. Let's take a look at these events in Job 1:13-22.

> One day when Job's sons and daughters were feasting and drinking wine at the oldest brother's house, a messenger came to Job and said, "The oxen were plowing and the donkeys were grazing nearby, and the Sabeans attacked and carried them off. They put the servants to the sword, and I am the only one who has escaped to tell you!"

> While he was still speaking, another messenger came and said, "The fire of God fell from the sky and burned up the sheep and the servants, and I am the only one who has escaped to tell you!"

> While he was still speaking, another messenger came and said, "The Chaldeans formed three raiding parties and swept down on your camels and carried them off. They put the servants to the sword, and I am the only one who has escaped to tell you!"

As if that's not enough, the shock continues:

> [Yet] while he was still speaking, another messenger came and said, "Your sons and daughters were feasting and drinking wine at the oldest brother's

house, when suddenly a mighty wind swept in from the desert and struck the four corners of the house. It collapsed on them and they are dead, and I am the only one who has escaped to tell you!"

At this, Job got up and tore his robe and shaved his head. Then he fell to the ground in worship and said:
"Naked I came from my mother's womb, and naked I will depart.
The LORD gave and the LORD has taken away; may the name of the LORD be praised."

"In all this, Job did not sin by charging God with wrongdoing."

Before we even get to our main points, I want to make sure we understand a basic premise of life—we must prepare to expect the unexpected. In the last chapter we discussed that this book of the Bible is not an easy walk in the park. The book of Job hits hardcore with real life. It's where the rubber meets the road. This is the reason why we are so drawn to the life of Job—it is exactly where everyone ends up at some point in life. No one is immune! Everyone will face surprises at some point in life's journey.

Let me share some good news about the unexpected before we go deeper into the details of Job's surprises. God doesn't want us to go through the valley unequipped. He has provided us with the book of Job to show us how to handle the unexpected. We are not alone! We often feel we are completely alone when we face trouble, but we can rest assured that God has provided us with real, raw examples to encourage us along the way. God's living and active Word equips us for all seasons of life. So to be well equipped, we need to look at some common threads of the unexpected we find in this passage.

Thread One—The unexpected often arises in the routine. Take a closer look at Job 1:13. "One day, when Job's sons and daughters were feasting and drinking wine at the oldest brother's house." They're just living life as normal. They gathered together as brothers and sisters to enjoy each other's company. We learned in Job 1:4-5 that they did this on a regular basis.

Not only was everything moving along as normal with his family life but everything was normal at work. Job 1:14 says, "A messenger came to Job and said, 'The oxen were plowing and the donkeys were grazing nearby.'" In other words, it's a normal day at work. A normal day with the livestock. A normal day on the farm. Everything is going just as planned.

Do you remember that at the beginning of chapter 1 we learned that Job was the wealthiest man in the area? He was the Bill Gates, Steve Jobs, Warren Buffet of the day. He had everything you could imagine. He had everything going for him. It's as if he owned the FedEx and UPS of the day because of the amount of camels listed in his portfolio. He had everything on a silver platter at this point. And then one day, while everything seems routine, the bombardment of attacks begins.

This is one of the pivotal points that connects our heart with Job's heart. Surprise will happen! We cannot calendar the unexpected. Life's going on as normal and then, in the midst of our routine, we're caught off guard.

Thread Two—The staggering surprise is often delivered by a messenger. Some of you can remember the moment a messenger came to you with an unexpected announcement. The doctor with your medical chart in hand! The phone call from a loved one! The letter delivered by the postman. The email notification sounding on your smartphone. A family member frantically calling about some tragedy that has happened in another family member's life. Regardless of your specific details, there has been a moment when a messenger arrives on scene. Four times in Job's story we read that "a messenger came."

Thread Three—The unexpected happens in the routine, appears via a messenger and finally the unexpected ambushes us. Have you ever used the phrase in your life "When it rains, it pours?" Maybe you have recently said under your breath, or aloud in the presence of others, clichés such as; "I can barely keep my head above water," "I feel like I'm just treading water," or "It all hit at once."

Did you notice the pattern the Bible reveals to us in this section of Job? Job 1:14 says, "a messenger came to Job." Two verses later in 1:16 we read that while one messenger was speaking another messenger interrupted him with more bad news. Job was not finished yet! In verse 17 and then once again in verse 18 we learn of other messengers.

The first messenger brought news of the loss of his oxen and donkeys that were carried off by a troop of enemy forces. While that messenger was delivering his news, the next one informed Job that his sheep and servants have been killed. The third messenger told of a raiding party stealing Job's camels. The forth messenger delivered the darkest news yet. It's the news a parent never wants to hear. All ten of Job's children have been killed as the house collapsed under the pressure of a mighty wind.

Pause for one moment and make sure you understand the gravity of what you just read. Job didn't lose just one child in a natural disaster, but ten. Seven sons and three daughters left this world in one sudden moment. The messenger said, "Your sons and daughters were feasting and drinking wine at the oldest brother's house, when suddenly a mighty wind swept in from the desert and struck the four corners of the house. It collapsed on them and they are dead, and I am the only one who has escaped to tell you" (Job 1:18-19).

Reasonable people certainly understand there will be difficulties this side of heaven. Jesus Himself stated, "In this world you will have trouble" (John 16:33). The problem is not a struggle here or there, but the turmoil which comes when life's struggles continue to pile up. If it's a good week and you are playing your "A game," you may be able to handle life's curve ball. One challenge at a time is doable. The problem many of us are facing right now is that struggles keep coming and coming and coming and coming. You feel ambushed and overwhelmed. This is the scene in Job's life. Before he can catch his breath from the first punch, another punch hits him from behind.

CHAPTER FOUR

Common Responses to Pain

Not only do we find common threads about the unexpected but there are also some common responses to the unexpected revealed in the book of Job. When pain sideswipes us from out of nowhere, there are several typical responses. Job is just like us. God can use the experience of Job to teach us about our possible responses to pain that may invade our lives.

Response one is "initial shock". The first five words of Job 1:20 state, "At this, Job got up." Don't ever overlook the details of God's Word, especially when you read a phrase like this one. It's very interesting to note that the preceding verses make no mention of him ever falling down. You can read chapter 1, verses 1 -19 and discover for yourself that the text doesn't record Job falling down, but it does record him getting up.

I believe scripture is clearly revealing to us that initial shock overcomes Job. Have you ever been in a situation where someone says to you, "You may want to sit down before I tell you what I'm about to share"? For instance, I have watched families at the hospital literally drop to the ground when a doctor delivers unexpected results from a surgery. Due to the heaviness of the event, there is nothing to do but fall to the ground. Sometimes a messenger delivers words so wrenching, they bring us to our knees.

I want to jog your memory about the human side of Job. He is not a superman. He's just a man. When the unexpected comes, we, like Job, are going to experience a typical human response. He was brought to his knees. The heaviness of the reports of destruction was a weight too heavy for one man's shoulders. It took him to the ground. Don't be surprised when the unexpected takes you to the ground. While down there, just get on your knees.

Beyond initial shock you will often see a second common response. Response two is "inner turmoil." As we read Job 1:20, we see that Job's next action was tearing of his robe. The act of ripping one's clothes is not a common practice in our culture today, but let's look at it from the perspective of Job's culture. Throughout the Old Testament in Middle Eastern culture, it was common for a person in grief to rip their robe as an outward symbol of their inner turmoil. Tearing an outer garment to shreds was reflective of their inner life being torn to pieces.

While the practice of tearing a robe may not be commonplace today, the imagery reflects the way grief makes us feel. When the unexpected strikes aren't you ripped to shreds? Wouldn't you say your heart feels torn and disconnected? This ritualistic act of an ancient culture speaks loudly to the pain you feel on the inside.

In my moments of greatest darkness I almost wish this cultural practice was acceptable in our modern day. Surely I'm not the only one who has felt like tearing something up because of the great pain on the inside. Unfortunately, I have observed too many people keep their pain bottled up on the inside. As the months and even years pass, bottled-up pain turns to bitterness. The inner turmoil begins to cross the line from healthy and a normal part of the grief process, to bitterness that eats away at the soul.

Is it time for you to tear your robe? Maybe you literally need to rip a garment as a method of moving pain from the lockbox of your heart to the open arena where it can be addressed. Maybe this biblical metaphor is enough to help you realize the need to open up. A man wearing a torn robe couldn't hide his pain from others. It was obvious that he was walking through a time of grief. Give yourself the freedom and permission to grieve. God sure does!

As if tearing the robe wasn't enough of an outward symbol of grief, we find there is more. Response three is "injured dignity." This response is noted in Job's action of shaving his head. Here's another practice of an ancient culture that seems unusual, but carries significant meaning in the grief process. The message of a shaved head was exposure. The hair that a person once had is now gone.

Isn't this the real issue with pain? Something we once had is no longer there. It could be a position, a possession, or a person. Loss jolts us into a new arena of life. This new way of life comes with a long list of unanswered questions. We may ask ourselves what we could have done differently. Deep grief can make us feel like less of a person. It can con us into thinking that the loss is our fault. Many grieving people blame themselves for issues over which they had no control. This injures our dignity.

So far, Job's responses have been very normal. Initial shock, inner turmoil and injured dignity seem like common menu items in the café of unexpected pain. The grief process in Job's life is progressing as normal. But fasten your seat belts because something abnormal is about to occur. This unique action of Job is the pivotal step that leads to ultimate healing.

As we continue through Job's actions as recorded in Job 1:20, we now arrive at an interesting turn of events. Here it is—Job has fallen to the ground once again. At first glance it may not be abnormal for someone to fall down numerous times under the weight of great pain. Collapsing once or twice or even a dozen times could be dubbed as standard procedure in light of the amount of loss Job faced.

Falling down in grief would be usual. But the Bible tells us that this act of falling to the ground was different. The text reads here that Job "fell to the ground in worship." The word "worship" changes everything. He isn't falling down this time out of uncontrollable grief, but as a deliberate act of worship. Friends, this isn't a common or normal part of our grief. But through the life of Job, God is teaching us a different way to handle pain.

Job has just faced utter devastation. Even after intense study of Job's life, I still can't wrap my brain around the magnitude of his sorrow. It's one thing to lose your material possessions. It's another, incomprehensible level to suffer the loss of all of your children in one sweep. With pain this deep, I find it remarkable that Job chose worship. The word "worship" in this text is a verb. It is action. Job, the grieving father and businessman, made a decision to worship God. It was an intentional act on his part.

To fully grasp the enormity of Job's action we need to have the proper understanding of worship. We typically think of worship as a once-a-week event that happens within the four walls of a church. If our only understanding of worship includes an occasional event of singing, giving, and preaching we are going to miss the thrust of God's message to us through Job's response.

The word "worship" literally means "to fall forward in submission to an authority." Don't rush too quickly past this definition. Worship means that we submit to God's authority. So what does Job do in the midst of unfathomable pain? He submits to the will of his Heavenly Father by falling to the ground in worship. The first three responses to the unexpected seem normal. This one seems radically abnormal. *Worship is the heal-*

ing ingredient in the unsightly batter of pain.

So what does this mean for you and for me? How does the right understanding of worship change difficult circumstances? Here's the paradox of this whole situation: Job weaves praise and pain together in the tapestry of seeming destruction. Chapter 1 of Job shows us some of the deepest pains of life. Job lost his entire livelihood. His business is now bankrupt. He lost his family—all 10 of his children are gone. His life is altered forever. He goes through initial shock, inner turmoil, and injured dignity. But he also worships God.

Specifically, according to the Old Testament understanding of worship, Job submits to God. Through this act of worship we can hear Job saying, "God, I don't understand all this. I don't comprehend the timing. I can't absorb the magnitude. But one thing I do know, I will submit to you. In the good, in the bad, in the up, in the down, in the pretty, and in the ugly, I will submit." This is what it means when the Bible says that he fell to the ground. Bible scholar, John Walvoord, says that Job fell to the ground "not in despair, but in obedience to God, Job worshiped."[1] The first time he fell to the ground in absolute despair. The second time he fell on his face in complete obedience.

Job was able to respond in worship to God because he understood the great qualities of God before the calamity struck. Since Job trusted God in the good times, he was able to cling to God in the bad times. His worship response is simply a natural outflow of what he already knew about God's sovereignty. A trust of God in the calm waters will prepare you for submission in the raging storms.

As we move forward in the passage to Job 1:21 we are now given clues to how Job was able to worship. The foundation on which Job's worship was built is revealed to the reader. I call these statements of authentic worship. The first statement of an authentic worshiper is "I submit to your will." We have already established that the word "worship" means to "submit to authority." It's an issue of reverence. Do I revere God? Do I release my desires so He can work His perfect plan in my life? This doesn't mean that in the center of turmoil we will always feel like singing songs. It doesn't mean that we're going to feel positive or ready to praise God. But it does mean that we will always submit to God regardless of the circumstance.

Many people believe that you only praise God when things are going well, or that you give God worship only if you feel like it. We often equate worship with a warm emotional feeling. Job's understanding of worship requires us to take a deeper look at our view of genuine worship. It is obvious in this context that worship is not associated with positive feelings and a joyful emotional experience. To the contrary, worship in this setting happens during the darkest valley anyone could fathom. God requires us to submit to His will in all situations. This is real worship!

Another statement of an authentic worshipper is, "I let go because it's all yours." Look what Job proclaimed in 1:21, "Naked I came from my mother's womb, and naked I will depart. The LORD gave and the LORD has taken away; may the name of the LORD be praised." Once again we are confronted with a radical declaration. Job has just lost everything and yet he cries out to God, acknowledging that nothing was ever his in the first place. Let this sink deep into your soul. Position, possession, and important persons in his life are gone and Job basically says, "It never was mine."

It's one thing if you talk about taking my position or possessions from me. Every possession you take away, I can replace. My replacement might not be as bright or colorful or shiny, but I can replace "things." But when you start talking about taking away loved ones, it gets personal. It gets raw. It gets real. We are pushed beyond what we believe we can handle when we address the loss of life.

This concept reveals the massive scale of Job's worship. Job has said to God, "Everything is yours. It has always been yours. You have the freedom to give and you have the ability to take away." You want to talk about authentic, radical worship? This is mega-worship. This is real worship. This is biblical worship. We truly worship God when we are able to say, "God, I entered this world with nothing. I leave this world with nothing. Therefore, it's all yours. I release everything back to you." What is your attitude toward God right now? Are you living with open hands or with closed fists? Some people have too tight a grip on the things of this world to take the step toward biblical worship.

There's a third statement of authentic worshippers found in this text. Job 1:22 reads, "In all of this, Job did not sin by charging God with wrongdoing." In other words, authentic worshippers say, "I will live right when everything is going wrong." All of us must make the choice of whether or not we're going to live right even when everything else is going wrong. Job chose to live a life of holiness in the midst of the horror.

Have you ever noticed our tendency to blame others? We become champions at pointing fingers when life goes wrong. The terrible turn of events in Job's life could have become a petri dish for blame. He could have even blamed God. After all, God allowed the darkness to enter his world. But the Bible tells us that Job did not charge God with wrongdoing.

I am convinced that Job was able to live right when everything went wrong because he made the decision to trust God when life was going well. He stood upright in tragedy because he was already standing upright when his life was on level ground. Don't forget that it was Job's regular custom to seek God. He sought purity in his personal life and on behalf of his family.

Are you willing to live right when everything goes wrong? The answer to that question will not be decided after the roof caves in but before. Today is your chance to surrender everything to God's will. Our view of God today paves the foundation for the season of storms. Picture for just a moment news footage of a neighborhood after a tornado. Debris may be scattered for hundreds of yards, but the foundation still stands. Since you know that storms will come, why not prepare yourself today by submitting to God? Nothing is ours. The time to acknowledge this truth is now.

Chuck Swindoll, in his book on Job, shares a story about a pastor friend of who forgot to take his suit to an important meeting. This is a humorous and true story that emphases the fact that we own nothing. Chuck writes:

> Ray once told me that he traveled to a site for a week-long series of ministry-related meetings. He had forgotten that there was a very nice evening dinner he was supposed to attend, and where he was scheduled to speak. When he had packed, he had failed to include a nice suit. He realized it towards the afternoon, when the hour was getting late.

Listen to this; it gets a little weird:

> Since his motel was located near a funeral home, he thought, "For just one evening, maybe the funeral director would be willing to loan me a suit," one that would later be used on a cadaver. He told

me that he went over to the funeral home and bargained with the director for a suit for that one night. Then he said this: "That evening, as I was addressing all the people, I did what I usually do. I reached up to put my hand in my pocket, but I couldn't. Right then, I realized that cadaver suits have no pockets."[2]

Naked we come into this world and naked we leave this world. None of it's mine. It's all God's. I'm going to leave earth with the exact same things I came in with…nothing except what has been given to me by the King of kings and the Lord of lords. Our response to difficulty will be based on our worship of God. Submit to Him. He's in control.

---

1   Walvoord, John F.; Zuck, Roy B.; Dallas Theological Seminary: *The Bible Knowledge Commentary: An Exposition of the Scriptures*. Wheaton, IL : Victor Books, 1983-c1985, S. 1:720

2   Charles R. Swindoll, *Job: A Man of Heroic Endurance* (Nashville, TN: The W Publishing Group, 2004), 26.

CHAPTER FIVE

Friendships That Ease the Pain

We have been looking at some really tough questions associated with pain, struggle and turmoil that affects us all at some point in life. We began by looking at the man of Job. The first test Job endured was the loss of all of his possessions, and his seven sons and three daughters. The second test he faced was a personal physical test. Now Job is stricken with boils and sores from the soles of his feet to the top of his head.

As we journey into the second half of chapter 2 we are introduced to Job's friends. These newly presented characters become a major part of the plot for the rest of the book of Job. We need to become familiar with the friends now because they are central to the rest of the story. Thirty-four chapters of this book are dedicated to the dialogue, or maybe I should say one-sided sermonettes, from the friends as they try to explain and justify the reason for Job's problems.

We will have time, in the coming chapters, to investigate many of the mistakes made by the friends, but our goal in this chapter is to learn how to become a friend who helps. I'm certain that all of us have experienced friendships that helped and friendships that hurt. If you are like most people you have friends you run to and friends you run from. I hope that you have had the joy of a friendship that is a constant help to you. If you haven't been surrounded by people who support and encourage you, perhaps this chapter will open your eyes to building healthy relationships.

The three brief verses of Job 2:11-13 provide us with a strong model for friendships that help. This ancient text has practical applications for healthy friendships in our modern day society. We are opening a passage that is thousands of years old, yet it has direct implications for friendships of the 21st century.

We live in a world where healthy relationships are hard to find. Backstabbing takes precedent over edification. Criticism is more prevalent than listening. Looking out for "number one" is elevated over seeking the best for others. It is my prayer that we will learn that somebody needs you and you need somebody. It seems that all people long for true friendship, but few know how to find and nurture friendships. Teaching us to become better friends is the goal of this chapter.

Let's join the next part of the story. Job 2:11-13 says,

> [When these friends] heard about all the troubles
> that had come upon him, they set out from their
> homes and met together by agreement to go and
> sympathize with [Job] and comfort him. When
> they saw him from a distance, they could hardly
> recognize him; they began to weep aloud, and
> they tore their robes and sprinkled dust on their
> heads. Then they sat on the ground with him for
> seven days and seven nights. No one said a word
> to him, because they saw how great his suffering
> was.

If we are truly going to be a friend who helps, we need to start by being intentional. This may sound elementary, but it is actually the cornerstone of great friendships. I know there have been times in my life God has laid someone on my heart or someone was brought to my attention, but I failed to act on that impression. Have you ever said to yourself, "I really need to give them a call. I really should run by to say hello." Or, "I really should send an e-mail or write a card of encouragement." *Great intentions lead to nowhere, but intentional steps can change a life.*

Hoping to change a life doesn't change a life. Impact requires action. But the problem is that your day gets busy. Then your week gets busy. And then you have four busy weeks, and a month passes. And before you know it, months have become a full year. Time really does fly, but few do anything to make their lives count.

A major lesson we learn from Job's friends is intentionality. The Bible says when the three friends heard about all the troubles that had come upon Job, they first set out from their homes. This shows an intentional step. Next they agreed to meet together. There's another intentional step. Then the scripture tells us they decided to go and sympathize with Job. Being there for Job wouldn't have happened without steps of intentionality.

Friends, we are called to reach out to others. God has designed us to be a blessing to others. We are not blessed to store the blessings for ourselves. God wants to allow blessings to flow through us. The flow of blessings will stagnate if we don't become intentional. We must take steps to encourage someone. Here's some homework to move you to action. Identify one person who needs ministry. Start with just one person. God may lay more than one person on your heart, but at least start somewhere. There will be someone in need this week who will cross your path. You can be the one who conveys a blessing to them. I want to encourage you to be intentional.

The second aspect to being a real friend is to simply be there. I know this sounds simple, but the simple is often profound. Real friends are there for one another. This doesn't mean that you know exactly what to say. Maybe you've never experienced their particular pain. Be there anyway. Maybe you don't understand what they are feeling. Be there anyway. Perhaps you can't relate to their current predicament. Be there anyway.

Often fear holds us back from being used by God. Is it possible you have withdrawn from a friend during a time of need because you fear you don't know what to say? Let me free you up from this bondage. The best friends are those who are just there. You may not know what to say. You may not know exactly how to deal with your friend's trial, but you can always be there. No excuses and no need for eloquent speeches. All that is needed is your presence. Now isn't that simple? We can all simply be there!

Along the same lines, did you notice the gravity of the situation when the friends arrived? Job 2:12 states, "When they saw him from a distance, they could hardly recognize him." Job was an absolute mess. This once wealthy and dignified gentleman now sits in the city dump among the ashes. The painful boils are so severe he has resorted to scrapping them with pieces of broken pottery. His friends were accustomed to him living in a large palatial surrounding, but now find him in a place for beggars. The sores from the top of his head to the bottom of his feet would cause anyone to question if this was really Job. As you continue to read the book of Job you will discover the despair in his soul. His entire countenance must have changed due to the great devastation.

Will you be a true friend to someone at their lowest point in life? It may be that your friend is behaving differently because of an illness. There are many sicknesses that can cause a person's appearance to change. Other struggles in life can cause a person's emotions to shift. You may find yourself using comments such as "Wow, that doesn't seem like them. That attitude is not typically him or her. That's not the way they normally look or normally act. That's not the way they normally sound." The challenges of life can alter a friend physically, emotionally, mentally, and spiritually. A real friend is someone who says, "I'm going to be there, even when you are in those moments in life that you just feel like everything's wiped out. When you are empty, I will be there to lift you up."

While we're on this topic, let's go a little deeper about the words we say. I have discovered that there are many well-meaning Christians who just don't know what to say. Fear of what to say can push us to different ends of the spectrum. Some persons avoid a hurting friend because they worry about getting tongue-tied and saying the wrong words. You have good intentions but choose not to reach out because you don't want to offend the person or embarrass yourself. The other end of the spectrum is the person who says too much. The over-talkers will be tempted to explain away their pain. There are moments in friendships, in marriage, in parenting, and in ministry when your presence is enough. Let God take care of the words. Simply allow yourself to be the vessel God will use.

Third, friends who help are wise. Did you note the detail in Job 2:13? The Bible states, "Then they sat on the ground with him for seven days and seven nights. No one said a word to him because they saw how great his suffering was." These friends show up at the lowest moment in Job's life and no one said a word to him for seven days. The friends have surveyed the situation and have chosen to remain speechless. I will warn you in advance that, in the next chapter, we will see that the friends eventually open their mouths. But right now, let's simply appreciate the wisdom of these silent friends. Keep your eyes open for those moments when your nearness is enough.

As we discuss wisdom, it's important to realize that explanations never heal a broken heart. You cannot fix pain with pat answers. Well-meaning people try to explain God or offer reasons for human struggle. Please be a real friend by using wisdom. When I think of what to say and what not to say, I am always drawn to James 1:19. This passage says, "My dear brothers, take note of this: Everyone should be quick to listen and slow to speak." A common flaw is that we often put the verse in reverse. We end up being quick to speak and slow to listen. Godly wisdom enables us to keep our speech in proper balance.

Another aspect of wisdom is the timeliness of the conversation. Have you ever been in a situation where someone said something to you that's very true, but it's just not timely? We must be careful to say the right thing at the right time. You may attempt to speak a truth that's biblically accurate and well-intended, but it's just not time for that truth in the friend's life. Don't hesitate to share scripture and encouragement. Just use judiciousness when it comes to the number of words used and the way you say them. At the moment of deepest pain, friends need your support more than your well-intended sermonette.

God recently laid on my heart the name of a pastor friend in South Carolina. I immediately called him and left a brief voice mail saying, "Brother, just want you to know, I appreciate your friendship. I'm praying for you right now." It wasn't much. Only a simple step of intentionality. A couple of days later I went to my office between our Sunday worship services and saw a text message on my cell phone. His text indicated that he was praying for me as I preached that morning. My phone call and his text message were very simple steps with profound impact. Knowing that another pastor is praying for me while I preach is a tremendous encouragement. Words were brief, but the impact was great. Intentionality will grow your friendships.

The fourth aspect of growing friendships is authenticity. Because life is difficult and filled with surprises, we will all have times of brokenness. There are going to be moments when you feel like you can't sweep up all the pieces of your broken life. Regardless of your status, background or position, all people will experience brokenness.

Unfortunately, some people don't like for others to see their brokenness. Plastic smiles replace real emotions. Putting on a mask is more common that opening up in front of a friend. Friendships thrive in an environment of authenticity rather than one of cover up. Remember that no one is perfect. This includes you and your friend. Share your life with others. Be vulnerable. Be real.

The passage in chapter 2 of Job shows us authenticity. Job 2:12 states, "When they saw him from a distance, they could hardly recognize him; they began to weep aloud and they tore their robes and they sprinkled dust on their heads." These friends acknowledged Job's and their own pain. They were completely authentic. They cried with him. They wept aloud.

There will be times in life when you just need someone to be authentic with you. If they break down and weep, that's fine. I love the passage in Ecclesiastes that states, "There's a time for everything. There's a time for healing; there's a time for sickness. There's a time to be mended; there's a time to be broken. There's a time to weep and a time to laugh." There's a time for everything. Real friends know when to laugh and know when to cry. They know when and how to mend and when to be silent in deep brokenness.

Authenticity also gives you the freedom to admit your limitations. There are moments where you must admit, "Look, I don't understand this situation." Don't pretend you understand. Just honestly admit you don't have an answer and you are wrestling with the issue yourself. By the way, this is not a sign of weakness. It's a sign of authenticity. On this side of heaven, no one will completely understand everything that happens. Real friends don't expect you to have all the answers. They are smart enough to know there's no way you will know everything. How can I be sure of this? They don't have all the answers either! Stop pretending. Be authentic!

The fifth attribute of helpful friendships is patience. Did you notice the detail, again, in verses 12-13? When the friends arrived, they mourned the same way Job mourned. First, they wept aloud. Second, they tore their robes. Third, they sprinkled dust on their heads. And finally, they sat on the ground with him for seven days and seven nights. No one said a word because of the magnitude of Job's suffering. The friends were extremely patient with Job.

As we apply patience in our lives, I want to encourage you in a couple of areas. First of all, would you be patient with your friend? Your patience will require time. This means that weeks, months, and maybe years may pass while you wait. Breakthroughs often take more time than we are willing to give. You may have to be patient through times that your friend seems cold or distant. You may have to wait while your friend erects barriers. It's even possible that your friend may get angry with you during the process.

I want to assure you that patience is worth it for one simple reason. We are patient with others because God has been patient with us. Even when I sin, when I mess up, in my flaws, in my repeated behaviors, God is patient with me. Knowing that God is graceful and patient with us should be the driving force in our patience with others. Even when the patience isn't deserved, God is there once again. Use God's patience as your model for waiting in friendships.

I would encourage you to be patient with yourself. You will mess up as you attempt to minister to others. We all do. There will be moments of misspoken words. Times will come when you wished you had done more. We all have instances when we are driving home after a conversation, replaying the entire dialogue and wishing we had said more or even less. Use wisdom. Learn from mistakes or opportunities missed but remember to be patient with yourself.

While we are talking about patience, we must also remember to be patient with God's work. You have to be patient with what He's doing. There is a mystery with God's work, but that doesn't mean He isn't working. Actually, God often does His best work in the silence. *An answer delayed doesn't mean an answer denied.*

A sixth and final point to healthy friendships is empathy. The latter half of Job 2:11 says the friends "met together by agreement to go and sympathize with him and comfort him." The word "comfort" in the Hebrew literally means "to shake the head" or "to rock the body back and forth." This word actually has very little to do with the words we say. It actually conveys how we feel.

Somebody today needs for you to be intentional. Somebody out there, through a phone call, through an e-mail, through a visit, through a card, through something, there's somebody somewhere who needs you to be intentional. There is a friend who needs you to be there. Someone in your family is looking for authentic concern. A work associate is longing for you to be real. There's someone in your life right now who needs you to be wise with your words.

Let me end this chapter with a closing question. Would you stop making excuses about being the type of friend that God wants you to be? There's somebody out there who's waiting for you to take a step. Maybe the issue is not in them coming to you but in you going to them. Are you willing to take a step to become that friend who helps?

CHAPTER SIX

Relationships that Increase the Pain

This chapter fits hand and glove with the last chapter on friendship. You have probably experienced the full range of friendships. You could say, "Yes, I've had some friendships that have meant the world to me. They've strengthened me. They've encouraged me. I've had friendships that help." But unfortunately the dark side of relationships is also a reality for many. Perhaps you've had times in your life when you must say, "I fall in the category of friendships that hurt. The one I thought I could trust betrayed me. When I was at my lowest point, my friend deserted me."

It is my prayer that these chapters on both sides of friendship will encourage you to restore a broken relationship. You can be the catalyst for change. But for change to happen you must take an honest look at mistakes you have made in the sphere of friendships. This chapter will help you learn from the mistakes of others. If we learn well we can avoid many of the friendship blunders we see in Job's friends. What a joy to know that scripture written thousands of years ago has direct impact on my life today.

Job's friends started out on the right path. The problem is they didn't continue doing what was best for Job. The first encounter with Eliphaz, Bildad and Zophar revealed caring friends who sat with Job in his darkest moment. They were authentic, patient, empathetic, and wise. Sadly, these wonderful qualities of friendship didn't last. Now, instead of sitting with him, we find them standing above him. Their religious piety and spiritual arrogance are released with fury on downtrodden Job.

I was recently reading a funny story about two friends on a hunting trip. By the way, I use the word "friends" loosely. Two hunting buddies went on a Northwestern United States expedition. While they're in the woods, suddenly one of the men yelled as he watched a grizzly bear charging at them. The first friend frantically put on his tennis shoes, and the friend anxiously asked, "What are you doing? Don't you know that you cannot outrun a grizzly bear?" And the friend said, "I don't have to outrun a grizzly bear; I just have to outrun you." I certainly hope you don't have any friends lacing up their shoes while a wild animal is seeking to devour you! In life there will be friendships that hurt.

Job's three friends ran out of patience and empathy. In the beginning they wept with him. They mourned with him. They started well. But it's what happens next that changes the course of their friendship. Thirty-four chapters of Job are dedicated to the conversations between Job and his friends. Beginning in chapter 4 and continuing through chapter 37, Job's friends attempt to set the record straight. Standing on the bully pulpit, they make accusations about Job's lack of faith and righteousness. Like a tennis match, words are volleyed between Job and his so-called friends. We have a bird's-eye view of this friendship gone bad. We must learn from their mistakes so our friendships can be strong and healthy.

Since we are dealing with such a large block of conversation, we are going to look at the themes that surface. Before we move forward, it is important to note the progression of this banter. If you take the time to read all thirty-four chapters, notice the tone of the dialogue as it progresses. It starts out as a mild discussion. There are no elevated emotions or verbal bombs at first. Then the tone moves toward heated debate. By the end of the exchange, they are in a verbal mud-slinging dispute. Tensions are high! Anger flares!

Reading those chapters of Job may remind you of our conversations today. Haven't you had discussions that start with mild discussion and end with harsh criticisms? God's Word is so relevant! The ancient words of what may be the oldest book of the Bible still ring true in our modern world. Human nature hasn't changed since the beginning of time. Our goal in this chapter is to learn from Job's friends' mistakes so we don't make the same mistakes.

One way we damage relationships is when we make incorrect assumptions. As you read the discourse, you will quickly unearth the friends' deficient theories about Job's plight. A clear example of this finger pointing is seen in Job 8:4-6. The text states,

> When your children sinned against him,
> he gave them over to the penalty of their sin.
>
> But if you will look to God
> and plead with the Almighty,
>
> if you are pure and upright,
> even now he will rouse himself on your behalf
> and restore you to your rightful place.

These chapters are written in poetic form. Let me cut to the chase with these verses. Basically, Bildad is telling Job, "Your children were sinners, and they deserved to die." Job has lost ten children and Bildad is hurling unjust accusations on his broken heart. Bildad continues by saying, "If you would only love God. If you would follow God. If you were pure in heart and lived an upright life, then you wouldn't be in this state of affairs."

Bildad's cold, heartless words are not based on accurate facts. Keep in mind what we learned in chapter 1 of Job. As the curtain opens at the beginning of Job we are presented with a holy and righteous man. Not a perfect man, but a God-fearing and God-honoring man. Job was so serious about holy living he would immediately offer a burnt offering on the behalf of his children after times of family gathering. He didn't want to give the enemy a foothold. Purity and holiness was Job's desire. This was his regular custom.

The accusation of Bildad is the epitome of the proverbial salt in a wound. Job is exposed; he is reeling from one of life's rawest moments both physically and emotionally. While at rock bottom, Bildad throws salt in Job's painful sores. The matter is even worse because the accusations are absolutely false.

As if the accusations aren't bad enough, we find that the false statements were prefaced with ugly insults toward Job. Job 8:2 records Bildad stating, "How long will you say such things? Your words are a blustering wind." This Hebrew phrase, "blustering wind," carries the same meaning as us saying, "You're just full of hot air." More directly, it would be similar to the statement, "You sound like an airbag." The friends are so high and mighty on their soapbox they have completely forgotten the agony in Job's heart.

Have you ever fallen into the trap of slinging false accusations? Is it possible that a fictitious hypothesis is the cause of your relational abyss? Please listen carefully to this next statement. You need to be very careful about assuming the will of God for someone's life. You can easily assume the position of God when you speak without caution. Too many relationships are broken at this moment because someone made incorrect assumptions about the activity of God.

In coming chapters, we will look more deeply at how God works, but I must at least state now that God's perfect will is too magnificent for us to fully comprehend. There is no way "finite" man can fully understand the work of our "infinite" God. There will be seasons in your life when you will feel like God is absent. Please remember that quiet moments don't mean God has deserted you. Don't falsely assume God has completed His work. Actually, I would encourage you to fasten your seatbelt while you are in the valley because God may be orchestrating a wonderful journey. Keep your facts straight and truthful. Don't speak falsehood to a friend about God's work in their life when you only hold a limited picture.

A second way we hurt our friends is through lack of verbal restraint. It's somewhat humorous that everything goes well when the friends are silent. They were great friends when they were grieving and empathizing. But when they opened their mouths, everything changed. Friends can get hurt when we lack verbal restraint. There are only two things that can come out of our mouths. We're either going to say something to bless others or curse them. We will either build them up or break them down.

A great example of a lack of verbal restraint is found in one of Job's rebuttals to Bildad. In Job 19:1-3 Job says, "Then Job replied, 'How long will you torment me and crush me with words? Ten times now you have reproached me; shamelessly you attack me.'" These verses clearly show that the friends didn't know when to stop. There were no brakes on the verbal assaults. Job states that he was beaten down verbally more than ten times.

Most of us are familiar with the old saying, "Sticks and stones will break my bones, but words will never hurt me." We all know this statement is absolutely false. I have watched people heal quickly from broken bones but spend a lifetime oppressed by the careless words of a close friend or relative. Job is accurate in saying that he was being crushed by the friends' words. Many people have recovered from all types of physical ailments, but still carry the scars of harsh words.

Is your life being influenced today by the cruel words spoken by someone in your past? It is not uncommon for a grown adult to carry the unkind words spoken by a parent. Many of the hang-ups people carry as adults stem from heated comments of a mother or father. For others, scars were formed by the words of a teacher or a coach. The unfortunate and typical pattern is that a false statement was made by someone who lacked verbal restraint, yet you allowed that untruth to become truth in your life. You have replayed that statement for so long you now assume it is correct. People who had the power to bring healing words to your life, delivered verbal lashings. Their lack of verbal restraint has inflicted you with additional pain on top of your original sorrow.

The Bible reminds us that we are to speak the truth in love (Ephesians 4:15). Some people prefer to speak the truth as a weapon, instead of as a tool of love. Without verbal restraint, we can become so focused on stating our viewpoint that we forget the pain of the one we are trying to help. Are your words tearing people down or building them up?

I recently found this poem called "The Builder." It makes us think about what we are actually doing with our words.

> I saw them tearing a building down,
>
> A group of men in a busy town.
>
> With a hefty blow and a lusty yell,
>
> They swung with zest,
>
> And a side wall fell.

Asked of the foreman,

"Are these men skilled? The kind you would hire if you had to build?"

He looked at me and laughed, "No, indeed. Unskilled labor is all I need.

Why, they can wreck in a day or two,

What it has taken builders years to do."

I asked myself, as I went away,

Which of these roles have I tried to play?

Am I a builder with a rule and a square,

Measuring and constructing with skill and care?

Or am I the wrecker who walks the town,

Content with the business of tearing down?

Your words are doing something. Are they building up, or are they tearing down?

A third way we hurt others is when we forget our own failures. As you study these passages you will notice the pattern of Job's so-called friends pointing out Job's failures. They accuse Job of moral malfunction. They charge him with a slack prayer life. They blame him for his condition by assuming Job doesn't seek God. These harsh accusations are a regular part of their sermonettes. Their talk makes one think that they have it all together. The friends are quick to point out the perceived failures of others without taking a look at their own lives.

An example of this is Job's reply in Job 12:3-4. Job states,

But I have a mind as well as you;
I am not inferior to you.
Who does not know all these things?

I have become a laughingstock to my friends,
though I called upon God and he answered—
a mere laughingstock, though righteous and
blameless!

Jesus taught on the issue of pointing out the faults of others with a great illustration. In Matthew 7:3-4, Jesus, the master illustrator stated, "Why do you look at the speck of sawdust in your brother's eye and pay no attention to the plank in your own eye? How can you say to your brother, 'Let me take the speck out of your eye,' when all the time there is a plank in your own eye?" We can hurt others when we point out their failures but forget our own mistakes.

A fourth way friends get hurt is when we attempt to work on them rather than walk with them. This is a major problem with Job's friends. Repeatedly the friends tried to "fix Job" instead of walking with him. Have you ever felt like a friend is trying to repair you instead of care for you? Sometimes friends make it their agenda to fix you. Although they may never say it directly, it seems like they are trying to fix your grief, flaws, or pain. This "fixing" is a major problem in many marriages. Instead of patience, love and support, a spouse can begin to act like a repairman. Make it a priority to walk with others. Love them. Pray for them. Listen to them. But make certain your goal is "walking with them," not "working on them."

I believe one of the reasons we try to quickly repair people is because our instant society has made us accustomed to quick fixes. We are now programmed to believe that anything can be fixed in ten minutes or less. Take a morning news show or afternoon talk show for example. Those shows often deal with major issues such as grief or parenting, but the "expert" attempts to give you all of the solutions before the commercial break. Immediately after the break, they move on to the next problem.

Or consider all the infomercials that blanket your television. You know the ones like perfect abs in 90 days. Or no more wrinkles in just one month with three easy installments to purchase the magic cream. Maybe you have been suckered into products that prepare your meals in seven easy minutes. Have you ever had your oil changed at Jiffy Lube? Why wait when you can have your car cared for in only half an hour? We are surrounded by a culture of rapid repairs. But friendships don't happen instantly. They require years of trust and investment. Since there aren't quick fixes for relationships, be sure to walk with others over the long haul instead of attempting to fix them. Relationships are more like a marathon rather than a hundred-yard dash.

In the middle of the accusations and replies, we find a specific request from Job. It's as if he has had enough of the repair job from his friends. Job speaks up and basically says, "This is what I need. I don't need you to figure me out. I don't need you to fix it. I don't need you guessing why God is doing what He's doing." It seems that Job has called a time out. Chapter 21 gives us Job's personal request.

Job says, "Listen carefully to my words; let this be the consolation you give me. Bear with me while I speak, and after I have spoken, mock on." He's begging for a break in the friends' painful monologues. He's basically saying, "Please listen to me, then you can mock on. But don't talk about difficulties in my life out of ignorance. At least listen to me." Then in Job 21:4-5 he states, "Is my complaint directed to man? Why should I not be impatient? Look at me and be astonished; clap your hand over your mouth." Job just acted on a thought that has passed through the mind of many. Have you ever wanted to tell someone to please put their hand over their mouth? Be sure to answer honestly.

Job's first request was for his friends to listen to him. Job says in 21:2 "Listen carefully to my words; let this be the consolation you give me." All of us long for someone to simply listen. In a world where everyone is talking and noise abounds, we just need a friend to listen. Don't pretend like you're listening and then try to solve with some pat answer. Remember, pat answers don't fix pain. They never have. Explanations do not heal a broken heart. They never will.

The Hebrew word for "listen" means "to listen with interest." Would that definition describe how you listen? Does your listening revolve around what you are planning to say next or is it focused on the person speaking? You have most likely heard before the phase, "That went in one ear and out the other." That expression is an unfortunate commentary on much of our communication. Real listening means that we listen with genuine interest. There must be sincerity with our listening if we are going to grow healthy friendships. Job's first request was simple. He just wanted someone to listen.

The second request found in Job 21:3 states, "Bear with me while I speak." This phrase takes Job's request to the next level. This is deeper than just listening. Actually the Hebrew word means "to carry or to pick up." So Job is begging for someone to help carry the pain for him. It's as if Job is saying, "Would you please pick up some of my broken pieces, instead of being the one causing broken pieces?" Job is crying out for his friends to carry the load instead of causing the load. A real friend, in the moment of crisis, is going to lighten the load instead of putting more on your shoulders. Job is saying, "I want someone who will listen to me with interest and carry some of the load for me."

The next request is found in Job 21:5. Job says, "Look at me and be astonished." What a simple but profound appeal. The Hebrew word for "look" means "to turn toward me." I want to suggest that Job's friends are no longer communicating with him face-to-face. Instead of looking Job in the eye, they may be looking at the ground or over his head. They have become so cold and distant it seems as if they now view Job as a project rather than a person. They may have close physical proximity to Job, but they are completely distanced emotionally. Job's petition is for his friends to look at him when they talk.

Haven't you been in a chat with another person and a few minutes into the conversation you want to shout, "Are you in the same room with me? Are you hearing anything I've just said?" Job must have felt the frustration of this scenario being played out in the exchanges with his friends. Let me encourage you to be aware of the way you communicate. It's been said that communication is over 70% body language. Our eye contact is certainly a critical aspect of body language. Don't get so passionate about stating your point that you look over the person. Your friendships can improve by simply looking at them sincerely when you communicate. Stay connected with the pain your friend is facing.

Friendships can hurt. Job has experienced the impact of friends with personal agendas and lack of concern. Learn from their mistakes. Perform a personal review of your friendship habits. You may be unaware of some damaging behaviors that God has exposed through the hurt caused by Job's friends. The bottom line in friendships is this: to be a vessel God can use in the lives of others. Don't act like you have all the answers. Your friends don't expect for you to provide all the solutions but they do need someone to walk alongside of them. Great friendships happen when you become a vessel for God instead of trying to play God.

CHAPTER SEVEN

The Underbelly of Unbearable Pain

Have you ever reached a point in your life where you said enough is enough? You have hit the wall. You are at the end of your rope and ready to throw in the towel. Life becomes so difficult you're not sure if you should laugh or cry. Rest assured you are among friends when you reach bottom. Everyone ends up between a rock and a hard place at some point of the journey.

This is exactly where we find ourselves now in the life of Job. He has hit his limit. And he expresses this openly and clearly. Yes, Job loves God. He is still a righteous man who has proven his trust in God. But he is human. In Job 3 we watch the floodgate of emotions pour forth. We are given a front row seat to the underbelly of unbearable pain.

This is the darkest chapter in the book of Job. It is certainly one of the heaviest chapters in the Bible. I don't remember memorizing any verses from Job 3 in Vacation Bible School. This chapter isn't making the front pages of daily devotionals. So don't expect a warm, fuzzy feeling after reading this section of Job.

But I personally like this chapter because it is real. Job makes some comments that verbalize the way you may feel right now. There's no easy way to tackle dark sorrow, but it is a reality we all must discuss at some point in life. It is my prayer that you will have the courage to face pain directly. Maybe you have tried to sweep it under the rug only to discover it never goes away. God has a purpose in His supernatural placement of this chapter in the Bible. Let's be open to God's message to us through Job's agony.

Before we embark upon this chapter let's recap the events that have brought Job to this place. Job lost all of his possessions. He has gone from being the wealthiest man in the region to abject poverty. He has been afflicted with painful sores from the top of his head to the bottom of his feet. He has lost seven sons and three daughters through a natural disaster. He has lost the support of his wife. Job 2:9 records his wife saying, "Are you still holding on to your integrity? Curse God and die!" The magnitude of destruction in his life is almost beyond our ability to comprehend.

As we prepare to read chapter 3, let's make sure we have it in the proper context. Job has been sitting outside of the city at the county landfill. His friends have come to join him. They sit with him for seven days and seven nights. Up until this place in the story, we have heard very little from Job. He has spoken few words and has just spent seven days in complete silence. Job's silence is about to change. Job 3:1 opens with these words, "After this, Job opened his mouth and cursed the day of his birth." I read this like a warning of coming events. Everyone take cover. Job is about to blow. Pain can only build up for so long before it overflows the banks of our souls. Here are Job's emotions put to words:

He said:

> "May the day of my birth perish,
> and the night it was said, 'A boy is born!'
>
> That day—may it turn to darkness;
> may God above not care about it;
> and may no light shine upon it.
>
> May darkness and deep shadow claim it once

more;
may a cloud settle over it;
may blackness overwhelm its light.

That night—may thick darkness seize it;
may it not be included among the days of the year
nor be entered in any of the months.

May that night be barren;
may no shout of joy be heard in it.

May those who curse days curse that day,
those who are ready to rouse Leviathan.

May its morning stars become dark;
may it wait for daylight in vain
and not see the first rays of dawn,

for it did not shut the doors of the womb on me
to hide trouble from my eyes.

Why did I not perish at birth,
and die as I came from the womb?

Why were there knees to receive me
and breasts that I might be nursed

For now I would be lying down in peace;
I would be asleep and at rest

with kings and counselors of the earth,
who built for themselves places now lying in
ruins,

with rulers who had gold,
who filled their houses with silver.

Or why was I not hidden in the ground like a
stillborn child,
like an infant who never saw the light of day?

There the wicked cease from turmoil,
and there the weary are at rest.

Captives also enjoy their ease;
they no longer hear the slave driver's shout.

The small and the great are there,
and the slave is freed from his master.

Why is light given to those in misery,
and life to the bitter of soul,

to those who long for death that does not come,
who search for it more than for hidden treasure,

who are filled with gladness
and rejoice when they reach the grave?

Why is life given to man
whose way is hidden,
whom God has hedged in?

For sighing comes to me instead of food;
my groans pour out like water.

What I feared has come upon me;
what I dreaded has happened to me.

I have no peace, no quietness;
I have no rest, but only turmoil."

You have just observed an emotional reservoir burst forth.
Raw honesty. No sugar-coated phrases. No beating around the

bush. Just a man and his words.

Also note that we have now moved into the poetry section of the book of Job. Therefore you will encounter repetition for the sake of emphasis. This is the way poetry works.

Pain is messy

Out of the sorrow and sadness in this chapter we want to gather some observations about unbearable pain. First of all, pain is messy. I know this may sound too simplistic, but I believe it is the perfect start to discussing this chapter. Frustration and disillusionment will consume your life if you believe that you are immune to messes. As one reads the words of Job we see how messy life can get.

Release yourself today by saying, "Life will have messes." Don't be shocked when life doesn't go as smoothly as you imagined. I believe that God allowed the events of Job chapter 3 to remind each one of us that life can and will be messy. Don't be afraid of the messes and don't be embarrassed to voice your emotions. The drive to appear as if you have it all together pushes you into a phony lifestyle. Too many people never address their issues because they plaster their face with an artificial smile. We pretend everything is going well and we become a master of cover-up.

I laugh when I think of the "cover-up" we attempt at our house when we discover someone is stopping by with short notice. You know that moment when someone is on their way to your home and you go into frantic clean-up mode. The game begins by cramming everything in a coat closet, under the couch or in the junk drawer. Or maybe you just use the technique of pushing stuff in the closest room and shutting the door. One of the joys of living in a two-story house is that we can make the downstairs look really nice for visitors while the upstairs could be best described as a disaster area. For some reason, we are driven to cover up messes.

At some point in your life, you are going to have to willingly accept messy. I know it may not fit the picture you want painted for your life. I understand that it's not the scene you would choose, but it is part of the growing process. Do yourself a personal favor today: accept messiness as a normal part of your spiritual development.

Along the same lines, isn't it interesting that Job's friends did not accept his messiness? Actually, thirty-four chapters of Job are dedicated to his acquaintances attempting to figure out or fix his mess. Their theory was that a righteous man couldn't have any messes in life. They assumed that people who follow God would have a perfect, shiny life with no streaks. With razor sharp words they tried to solve Job's mess. Don't be dismayed by chaos in life. Also, don't think you deserve a free pass because of your level of righteousness. Have no fear. There's nothing wrong with you. God uses all things for His glory.

Pain causes questions

A second observation for this chapter is that pain will cause you to ask questions. Did you notice all the questions Job asked throughout his monologue? Here are some examples: Why did I not perish at birth? (v. 11) Why was there someone there to receive me? Why was there a mother there to nurse me? (v. 12). Why was I not hidden in the ground like a stillborn child? (v. 16) Why is light given to those in misery? (v. 20) Why is life given to a man whose way is hidden, who God has hedged in? (v. 23) Pain has a way of bringing out some of life's most challenging questions. Give yourself room to ask questions.

Please understand that asking a question doesn't always mean you will get an immediate answer. It is common for God to remain silent during the testing. But doesn't this make perfect sense? Let's think for a moment about tests we take in school. When you're in the midst of taking an exam, your professor is not going to give you the answer. You may repeatedly raise your hand and beg for an answer, but during the test you may not get the answers.

Before the exam, the teacher should have prepared you for what's coming. Additionally, a serious student would be prepared for the test because a student would expect testing as a regular part of development. But in the midst of the testing we rarely get the answers. In school I remember my favorite teachers would debrief me after the test on ways to prepare for the next test. This way I could learn from my mistakes in that test and be better prepared for the next one.

This is certainly similar to God's pattern of spiritual development for us. If we are growing in our walk with God, then we are preparing for upcoming tests. Each day as we spend time in God's Word and in prayer we are getting prepared for the next time of testing. Then when the testing comes, we are not shocked that there may be a time of silence. It's certainly okay to ask questions, but we must realize that God will provide everything we need to know in His timing, not ours. God's answers may be mysterious, but they are always right. Correct in timing and correct in the information provided. There are some questions that will not receive complete answers this side of heaven.

Pain causes "if only"

A third observation of unbearable pain is that it can lead you to reconstruct events. Did you catch what Job was doing in this passage? He was wishing he could remake time gone by. In reference to the day of his birth, Job states, "That night— may thick darkness seize it; may it not be included among the days of the year nor be entered in any of the months (3:6)." In other words, he was begging God to take his birthday off the calendar.

This is very similar to playing the "if only" game. You know those times in life when you become consumed with the emotionally and physically draining struggle of trying to make things different. Typical statements such as, "If only we would have been five seconds earlier. If only I wasn't at that intersection when that other car ran through it. If only I wasn't on that four-wheeler at that moment. If only we didn't go swimming at that moment." The phrase "if only" is our attempt to recreate events. This is exactly what Job's trying to do. His specific request is "If only God would take the day of my birth off the calendar."

I was recently listening to an interview on a radio station with Lou Holtz. They were asking him about many of the successes throughout his coaching career. He stated that his coaching philosophy could be summed up with an acrostic for the word "WIN." It stands for "What's Important Now?" He went on to say, "Each Sunday morning, I can watch every play we executed on Saturday. I can watch every quarter. I can watch every moment. But do you know what? I cannot go back and change any of those plays. They're done. I can scream, I can shout, I can throw my fists around, I can do anything I want, but I cannot change yesterday's plays." The winning strategy is to focus on what's important now.

Many people have their finger stuck on the rewind button. You want to reconstruct events in every moment of your life. You think over past events that can never be replicated. Let the past teach you, but not overwhelm you. The unhealthy habit of reconstructing the past takes much needed energy away from the present.

Fourth, we must understand that just because pain shows up does not mean you messed up. Could I remind you of something about Job? He is a righteous man. He feared God and shunned evil. When God was in dialogue with the accuser, Satan, God stated twice, "Job is a man who honors me. He is a man who fears God. He is a man who lives right." Matter of fact, the scripture revealed that Job interceded for his children. He did not want one hint of sin in his family's life. Job loved God. He was a man of faith.

Job loved God so much that, even after losing his children and every possession, his response was; "I didn't come into the world with anything. I'm not walking out of this world with anything. The Lord gives, and the Lord takes away. I bless the name of the Lord" (1:22). When his wife came to him and said, "How can you still follow God? How can you still love God? How can you do this?" Job's response was, "Can we accept good from God and not accept trouble?" Job trusted God. He lived right and pain still showed up. Pain's presence doesn't suggest that you have failed.

Unfortunately, Job's friends equated pain with disobedience. They assumed there were loopholes in his righteous living. Armed with their flawed hypothesis, they started an investigation into the source of Job's pain. They interrogated him like a criminal. Accusations of sin and unrighteousness became their weapon of choice. Instead of accepting pain as part of God's will and work in Job's life, they were determined to surface Job's transgressions.

Please listen closely to the following statements. First, the presence of pain does not mean the absence of righteous living. Second, the presence of pain does not mean the absence of God. There are times that pain shows up in our life because God loves you so much and He wants to show us more of Himself. He often uses discomfort to speak directly to us. And if the truth were told, we can be very stubborn. Pain and the accompanying uneasiness can be a powerful tool to get our focus off of ourselves and onto God.

A fifth observation of unbearable pain is that pain and faith can coexist. Just because you have pain doesn't mean you lack faith. The scriptures show us that Job had great faith, yet he had overwhelming distress. Job had faith and he had questions. There was even faith and frustration.

As you read Job 3, you can feel the helplessness. Out of this season of raw vulnerability, he voices his emotions. Life as he knew it is gone. It will never be the same again. Job feels completely helpless and doesn't hesitate to articulate his honest sentiments to God. But he still hangs onto hope. Helpless, yes! Hopeless, no!

There will be moments in all of our lives when we feel helpless. But don't equate that to mean that you are hopeless. Job is a great man of faith. But the key word is "man." He is a human being who has hit his limit. And even though he expresses the hurt in his soul, he does so without ever cursing God. He wishes the calendar could be different. He expresses his frustration. He even desires to turn back time. But he never once curses God. Is he helpless? Absolutely. Does he hurt? In ways we'll never understand. Does he show anger? Absolutely. Is he frustrated? You'd better believe it. But never once does Job curse the name of God.

I want you to know that pain and faith can co-exist. The presence of pain does not mean you're messed up. Actually, it may mean you are right on track in your faith pilgrimage. We should be encouraged that God allowed Job and many other biblical heroes to face pain. He used those moments to refine them. Remember that God is more than able to work with faith the size of a mustard seed. Pain is not an oddity, but a necessity. It's one way God enables us to know Him better.

CHAPTER EIGHT

When the Storms Lift

We have hurt with Job as we watched him face great adversity. The trials have been numerous. The pain has been agonizing. His wife thought it was better for him to die. His friends were sure sin and rebellion was the cause of his angst. And the worst part… God seemed silent.

But now we are drawn to the edge of our seats because God is about to speak. Will God side with the friends? Is Job finally going to get the answers to his questions? Will the purpose behind Job's pain be revealed?

After thirty-four chapters of dialogue between Job and his friends, God begins to unveil His perfect plan. God allowed Job to vent in chapter 3. The friends had more than enough time to voice their opinions of the situation. But it's now time for a new tone. As we enter into chapter 38, the scene changes. The stage has been reset, the curtain rises, and now the key player in this story is front and center.

The first verse of Job chapter 38 simply says, "Then the Lord answered Job out of the storm." This had to be a surreal moment for Job. Out of the storm, God Almighty speaks. Job has cried out to God and has waited. He has endured the verbal lashings from others and has waited some more. He has weathered the storm. Now he gets to hear from God.

God's answer begins in chapter 38 and continues through chapter 41. But before we look at the details of God's reply to Job, we need to understand one overarching quality about how God works—God's answers will always point you to more of Himself. I find it interesting that God doesn't give specific answers for every question Job asked. God doesn't attempt to explain the pain. He simply wants Job to see more of Him.

For some, this approach to answers is troubling. We often demand answers and want the details of "why." The bottom line is that God is God. He isn't required to reply to all of our inquiries. Actually, the real answer will never be found in our curiosities being satisfied. God reveals to Job that He is enough. You many never get all the details to the "whys" of this world. By the way, we should be glad that God doesn't give us all the specific information about every situation in life. We could never take it all in. But we can learn to be completely satisfied with who God is. This is God's answer to Job. God is saying, "Job, I am the answer. I've always been the answer. I've always been there with you, but there are some things that you missed. So the answer is more of me."

We all know that on this side of heaven we will not have all the answers to life's difficult questions. No one has the answers except God. There will always be mystery surrounding the ways of God. This certainly shouldn't come as a surprise since God sees the whole picture while we are limited by location and time. But when we understand more about the character of God, we will understand more about the way He works and the way He answers. For this reason, we want to investigate four foundational characteristics of God revealed through His response to Job.

God is always present

The first characteristic is His omnipresence. This simply means that God is always present. Look at what God said in Job 38:4-7:

Where were you when I laid the earth's
foundation?

Tell me, if you understand.

Who marked off its dimensions? Surely you know!
Who stretched a measuring line across it?

On what were its footings set,
or who laid its cornerstone—

while the morning stars sang together
and all the angels shouted for joy?

God wants Job to understand that He has been present before Job ever arrived on the scene. God answers by saying, "You weren't there when the foundation of the earth was laid. You weren't there when I measured out and marked off where the land stopped and the water starts. You weren't there but I was. I have always been present." You can't understand how God works if you don't first recognize that God has always existed and He's always present.

God's silence is not the same as God's absence. Yet you may be wrestling with God because you believe He is not involved in your pain. We must understand that God's silence doesn't mean His absence. He is always present in your life. This is a promise repeated throughout the Bible. Don't forget the example about a teacher during times of testing. The teacher is right there with you even though he may be silent during the time of the test. God is the Alpha and Omega. In other words, He is the beginning and the end. When you feel alone rest in the knowledge that God is always present.

God is all powerful

The second character trait God reveals to Job is that He is all powerful. This is His omnipotence. Look at Job 38:24-30.

> What is the way to the place where the lightning
> is dispersed,
> or the place where the east winds are scattered
> over the earth?
>
> Who cuts a channel for the torrents of rain,
> and a path for the thunderstorm,
>
> to water a land where no man lives,
> a desert with no one in it,
>
> to satisfy a desolate wasteland
> and make it sprout with grass?
>
> Does the rain have a father?
> Who fathers the drops of dew?
>
> From whose womb comes the ice?
> Who gives birth to the frost from the heavens
>
> when the waters become hard as stone,
> when the surface of the deep is frozen?

Basically God is saying, "Who are you to think that you would know the origins of lightning? Who are you to think that you cut the channels for rain? How can you know when something should freeze or thaw?" God provides specific details to showcase His power. The Almighty wants Job to understand that man is limited in power, but God is all powerful and unlimited.

God uses tests to remind us of our limitations. As you are

stand in the midst of the valley you may say, "I don't have the power to get through this. The valley is too deep and wide for me to overcome." You believe that you don't have the strength to make it another day. Throwing in the towel seems like the only option.

At the moment when Job feels lifeless and powerless, God speaks. In a nutshell God is saying, "Let Me remind you that I am in control of every detail of life." God reminds Job that the rain, lightning, frozen ground, and melted ground are all under His control. He even goes on to say, "Job, it's not you who fathers the dew. It's not you who fathers the rain. It's Me." If we really understand that God is sovereign over every detail of nature, we can live confidently that He is ruling over every detail of our lives.

I've got great news for you! First, you need to understand God is always present, even if life makes you feel like He's absent. There will be times you may not see the work of His hand, but you can always trust the plans of our Father's heart. Second, you need to understand that His power is great enough for every detail of your life. God overlooks nothing. God wastes nothing. His power and presence is enough. This is great news!

God is all-knowing

The third character trait revealed to Job is that God is all-knowing. The theological term is God's omniscience. We have just watched as God took Job on a walk through nature (chapter 38). The tour included a look at the clouds, storms, lightning, and frozen tundra. Now, God takes Job on a walk through the zoo (chapter 39). Look closely at chapter 39:1-4:

"Do you know when the mountain goats give
birth?

Do you watch when the doe bears her fawn?

Do you count the months till they bear?
Do you know the time they give birth?

They crouch down and bring forth their young;
their labor pains are ended.

Their young thrive and grow strong in the wilds;
they leave and do not return.

The sightseeing trip through the zoo continues through the entire chapter. For example, 39:9 says, "Will the wild ox consent to serve you?" Again God asks, "Do you give the horse his strength or clothe his neck with a flowing mane?" (39:19). In 39:26-27, He asks, "Does the hawk take flight by your wisdom and spread its wings toward the south? Does the eagle soar at your command?"

God's telling Job, "Were you the one who figured out what horses should wear and what they should eat? Are you the one who gave the horse the strength? Do hawks fly because of your design?" God goes to great lengths to make sure Job discerns that only God knows what's best for all the animals.

God is intimately involved with the mane of a horse, the feathers of an ostrich, and the labor pains of a mountain goat. He cares about His creation and cares even more about you. There is not one detail of your life that has been overlooked. God sees all and works through all. He really knows all.

The answer that satisfies is not intellectual but relational. To find peace in the answers to life's tough questions, you must first personally know the answer maker. God is showing Job that the answer is not found in human reason, but in an all-knowing God. God is the answer! He created and He cares. God's answers are always going to point us, first and foremost, to more of Him.

God's answers also point us to less of ourselves. Let me take you back to Job 38:2. This verse states, "Who is this that darkens my counsel with words without knowledge?" God is telling Job that he may have words which attempt to explain the struggle, but only God has the knowledge. It's as if God is saying, "Job, you don't have all the answers. You need to be in your place; I'll be in My place." Human words are limited. God's knowledge is complete.

We see signs that Job is beginning to understand that God is the answer through his comments in Job 40:4. Job states, "I am unworthy—how can I reply to you? I put my hand over my mouth." There is a key word in the passage we must not overlook. The word is "unworthy." Some translations may say "insignificant." Regardless of the English word used, the important factor is the original meaning in the Hebrew. The Hebrew word literally means, "light in weight." Now, grasp this for a minute. Take time for Job's response to sink into your own heart. If I read this with the literal Hebrew word the passage says, "I am a lightweight." That's literally what it means. "I am a lightweight—how can I reply to you?"

One of the reasons we don't always hear from God like we want to hear from God is because we think too much of ourselves. We think we've got life all figured out. We spew out comments such as "God, I really wish You would have placed this testing at a later place in my life. God, you should have put this difficulty somewhere else on the calendar. God, this one doesn't fit my agenda." We start telling God what to do and what not to do. We act as if we are the heavyweight. But in reality, we are just a lightweight.

Job's next breakthrough of understanding is found in Job chapter 42:3. The passage states, "You asked, 'Who is this that obscures my counsel without knowledge?' Surely I spoke of things I did not understand, things too wonderful for me to know—things too wonderful for me to know." These are the words flowing from a transformed Job. He now gets God's answer.

Remember not long ago in our study we heard Job saying, "What about the justice? Why did I even have to be born? Why are you shedding light on my sorrow?" Job was crying out with the common question of "why?" Now, Job's a new man. The clouds are lifting. The storm is over. The answer is clear. The problem wasn't with God. The problem was with Job's understanding. He misunderstood his place and overlooked God's position. Now Job's saying, "Okay, I get it. I'm a lightweight. Surely I spoke of things I did not understand. Surely I spoke a bunch of words without knowledge." He surrendered his limited view to God's eternal, all-knowing, and all-powerful perspective.

Job is waving the white flag saying, "Father, I cannot answer. You're exactly right. I cannot fathom things that You're trying to do. I wave the white flag of surrender and I admit that I have thought too much of myself." If you want to experience a movement of God in your life and if you want to see God do a mighty work through you, the best thing you can do is surrender. Come before Him and say, "Father, I am a lightweight. I come in humility before You. Forgive me for trying to play God. You are the only God. You are in control of all seasons in life." The ultimate answer in life always points to more of God. Every time God answers us, it's going to point to less of ourselves and more of Him.

God's answers also point us to an eternal perspective. A major problem for us as we live on this earth is thinking only in the realms of this present world instead of looking through eternal lenses. Let's look at Job 38:33. God asks, "Do you know the laws of the heavens? Can you set up God's dominion over the earth?" In other words, He's trying to get Job to see that He doesn't work in minutes, weeks, or years. God is not bound by our view of time. God has always done, and continues to do, His work from eternity to eternity. Don't forget that God is the Alpha and Omega. Our Heavenly Father sees the beginning and the end. There is so much more at work in our little world than what we can see.

During one of the sermons I preached on Job, I showed my congregation a series of four pictures. The first one was a photo from the front of our church sanctuary. The angle was from the front steps of the building looking up toward the steeple. It was a picture with a limited view. From a ground perspective you can only see a short distance before the sight lines end.

The next picture was from Google Maps showing our church facility from an aerial view. It was similar to the view I saw as my Delta Connection flight approached the Asheville Regional Airport. As I looked out of the window of the aircraft, I could see all of downtown Hendersonville, NC, and a very clear perspective of the church campus. It was a completely different view from the one standing in front of the church.

Then I revealed the third picture. It was a picture of planet Earth taken from the Space Shuttle. Of course, this wasn't a photo from my digital camera, but one of those photos of the entire world. It was a picture from a perspective which I have never seen with my own eyes. There are some astronauts who have seen our world from this perspective, but most of us haven't had that privilege. It is a grand view that is out of this world.

Finally, the fourth picture illumined the screen. It was a photo taken by satellites revealing the shape of the Milky Way galaxy. This is, of course, a view no human has seen in person, but a perspective God sees every split second. As a matter of fact, every time we build bigger satellites and bigger telescopes, we find millions of undiscovered stars and vast galaxies beyond our imagination. There is so much more than our eyes can see. Shame on us for thinking the only perspective is the one just before our eyes. One of the reasons that God allows us to go through trials is because He wants us to see from an eternal perspective.

Along the same lines, God's answers will always point us to less of a temporal view. In Job 42:2 Job states, "I know that you can do all things; and no plan of yours can be thwarted." After all of Job's wrestling, frustration, anger, pain, and suffering, this is Job's final conclusion on the matter concerning God's ways. He realizes that nothing can foil God's plans. The loss of possession, position or people cannot short-circuit the will of God. Our temporal view keeps our focus on the loss. God's eternal view opens our eyes to heavenly purpose.

I'll never forget a flight we took a few years ago with three of our children. At the time my youngest was too little to travel. We boarded a smaller, regional jet in Charlotte for a trip to Detroit. It was the first flight for my youngest daughter, Victoria. We boarded the plane as usual and got settled in our seats. Just a few minutes after boarding while we were still parked at the gate, we felt a strong bump. It felt like something hit the aircraft causing it to move slightly. I looked out of my window and noticed that one of the large luggage carts used by the baggage handlers on the tarmac had rolled away from the convoy of carts. Unfortunately, it actually became lodged under the wing of that smaller plane causing damage to the wing.

After a few minutes of attempting to dislodge the cart, the captain announced over the PA system that we needed to exit the airplane so they could get a new aircraft. I'm glad they realized the need for a new plane instead of trying to make repairs with duct tape! I prefer to fly in planes without damaged wings. Anyway, we had only been on the plane parked at the gate for ten minutes or less.

Remember that my young daughter had never flown before. She had no perspective of flight. As we walked back through the jet walk, Victoria, in a sweet, innocent voice asked, "Are we already there?" She thought that ten easy minutes sitting on a plane got you to your destination! Here's what I realized about Victoria and that moment—she had no perspective from which to evaluate a situation she had never experienced. She didn't know what it felt like to feel a plane power up at the end of the runway and obtain the speed necessary for takeoff. She had no way of knowing what it feels like to soar in the air when the plane reaches cruising altitude. She had no idea what it felt like to land at her final destination. She could only see life from that ten-minute perspective.

Here's the application from that event. Often we complain to God about a situation concerning which we have no perspective. We are living life from a completely different view. We have to trust that God knows what's best in all circumstances. He is trying to teach us to see things from His perspective, not our limited perspective.

God always answers with more of Himself. God always answers by reminding us that it needs to be about less of me. God always answers by showing us a bigger picture of eternity. And God always answers by pointing us to having less of a temporary, temporal view.

I know it's difficult to keep the right perspective during the storm. The straight line winds and driving rains can impede our view. Our focus during these times must be on the One in charge of the storms. And we can fully trust that, at just the right time, He will speak out of the storm. Remember Job 38:1 says, "The Lord answered Job out of the storm." Remain confident that God will do the same for you!

CHAPTER NINE

Rebuilding the Broken

Although this book has investigated the question "why," another closely related question is always looming. The pressing question right around the corner is "when." Haven't we all looked into the heavens and exclaimed, "Father, when am I going to see the broken rebuilt?" Most people are not naturally patient. Therefore, we are always wondering when things are going to change.

But the questions don't stop there. Standing in queue right behind the question "when" is the question "how." As you look at the broken pieces in your life you wonder how the mess could ever be restored. From our view, we don't see solutions for people who refuse to change, situations that look impossible, and relationships that appear destroyed. How could anything good ever come out of so many broken pieces?

If you have wondered how God could ever overhaul your life, then you have arrived at the right place in scripture. If you think it's all over for Job, then read on until the end of the book. Job 42:7-16 reveals the hope and healing we long to see in his life and ours. Welcome to the place that reminds us there is hope. Extreme makeovers aren't just television dreams. They are God's specialty! He really does rebuild the broken.

Our "instant" culture has programmed us for on-the-spot results. High-speed internet is too slow. One minute in a fast food drive-thru seems like an eternity. One-hour photo? Who needs it when I can do everything instantly with a digital camera and personal computer! We now have an entire generation that believes instant gratification is a birthright. Unfortunately, we have put the same expectations on God. Yes, God rebuilds, but He may not do it on our timetable.

I call this the "light switch" mentality. One flip of a light switch and a darkened room is immediately illuminated. This isn't an unreasonable expectation in our modern society but it can become unreasonable if we impose the same standard on God. God can, and often does, work immediately. He is God Almighty who spoke the world into creation. He wanted light and He spoke in into existence. He is completely capable of doing things immediately.

But God most commonly works over time. Think once again about the creation account. He spoke it and it happened, but it was over a period of six days. He could have done it in one day or one split-second, but God chose to create over time. God did mighty work in the lives of Abraham and Moses, but it was over a span of years, even decades. God's greatest work through His own Son, Jesus Christ, occurred over time. Jesus lived 33 years. Thirty of those years were spent in preparation for his ministry. Also remember, for three days the world thought Jesus was destroyed and God's plan was stopped. But then, three days later, God showed His finishing work through the resurrection.

Now back to our brief lesson in interior illumination. Light switches are one way to brighten a room. But don't forget about dimmer switches. They also illumine but do it over a period of time. It seems consistent with God's pattern that He will often illuminate our situations over an interval of time.

I have discovered, through God's Word and through my own life experiences, that God reveals just what we need to know at each point in life. As we take steps of faith, God sheds more light on what we need to know. God's work in us and on us is a process. Patience is required and is one of the ways God recreates us during the rebuilding process.

Let's get back to our story of Job. This man's brokenness made such a mark in history that we describe someone suffering as a "modern day Job." Job's pain has been unfathomable. It staggers our imagination to even attempt to comprehend what he has faced. But here's the good news of Job's story: *God can take a mess and make a message.*

Don't forget the magnitude of Job's mess. Here's the debrief: loss of material possessions, the tragic death of all ten of his adult children, agonizing illnesses, abandoned by his wife, beaten down by his friends, and, most troublesome, is the unknown reasoning behind God's purpose. Some of you have been there, too. You have suffered physical pain or suffered financial loss. Some of you have faced the bottom of the barrel financially. Many of you have dealt with tremendous physical ailments and pain. Others can relate to the abandonment.

Repentance

So how does this rebuilding process work? Well, first of all, we are fooling ourselves if we think God is going to rebuild the pieces in our lives unless we take the first step of repentance. This was the first brick of the rebuilding process in Job's life. In 42:6 Job states, "Therefore I despise myself and repent in dust and ashes." God will not reconstruct your life if you are holding the construction equipment. Job's statement is one of absolute surrender. He knows that rebuilding will be accomplished God's way, not his. Job lays down all of the pieces so God can begin the rebuilding.

Another testimony of surrender is found in Job 42:2. "I know that you can do all things; no plan of yours can be thwarted." Job acknowledges that human reasoning is never the answer. Didn't we hear enough of man's strategizing through the friends' monologues? Job learned that real repentance is laying down all of life's pieces. When we fail to repent, we are holding back some of the pieces God will use in the rebuilding process.

Are you ready to come before God and admit that you don't have life all figured out? Will you accept the fact that you don't see all the pieces but God does? What is really holding you back from trusting God completely? It may be something from 20 years ago. It may be something from 20 minutes ago. It may be a person. It could be an agenda or vendetta lurking in your heart. Regardless of what it is or how old it is, it must be confessed and surrendered to God.

I love the story that I read about Norman Vincent Peale in his childhood. As a child, he would sneak some of his father's cigars and try to find a secret place to smoke them. His father reprimanded him numerous times. He finally got into the habit of going in the alley thinking his father would never find him. One time, while smoking in the alley, his dad came outside and saw the billowing smoke around the young Peale. Norman quickly placed the cigar behind his back thinking he could hide it from his dad. So the young Peale tried to divert his father's attention by focusing on a billboard advertising the coming circus. Norman says, "Hey Dad, look at that billboard. Can we go to the circus?" Norman Vincent Peale writes of his father's response, "My dad said quietly but firmly 'Son, never make a request while at the same time trying to hide a smoldering disobedience.'" Is it possible that we are delaying the rebuilding process because we are requesting things from God while holding a smoldering disobedience behind our back?

Restoration of relationships

We discover that the next step in this rebuilding process is the restoration of relationships. I want to propose to you that this is actually a third test in Job's journey. The first test was revealed in chapter 1. The loss of all of his possessions and the death of his children was the first test. The second test was the physical ailments. Boils covered his body from the bottom of his feet to the top of his head. Descriptions of the symptoms listed through the book of Job could easily make one sick at his stomach.

But now we are brought to what I would like to call a third test. The reason I believe it's very appropriate to call it a third test is because now Job is being asked by God to be the conduit of restoration for his friends. There are many difficult circumstances in life, but relational brokenness may be at the top of the list. As a pastor, I have walked with many church members through shattered relationships. Words can hurt. It is incredibly difficult to let go of harsh words spoken toward you. But Job is now asked to pray over his friends when they come to him. These are God's instructions.

In Job 42:8, God says, "So now take seven bulls and seven rams and go to my servant Job and sacrifice a burnt offering for ourselves. My servant Job will pray for you, and I will accept his prayer and not deal with you according to your folly." Do you see that God's restoration plan involves Job? Job is called by God to be the vehicle for grace to the very ones who lack grace.

God is saying to Job, "You know those friends who threw you under the bus? Remember those closest to you who turned their back on you. You know the friends who said you were full of sin and not living correctly? I am going to use you to restore them." This is truly a major test. I am convinced that is a test of his repentance. Often we will tell God that we are sorry for stepping out of place, but they are only empty words. The real test is our actions after we repent. Do our behaviors actually change? Is there such a difference in our attitude that it merges with our actions? So the real test is when we do repent do we mean business?

Immediately following Job's repentant statements, God put Job to the test. Job's eyes were open to God's plan for his life, but was his heart open to real change? We know we are transformed when we are willing to pray for those who aim to harm us. The ones who beat Job down are now to be lifted up to the Heavenly Father by Job himself.

God is a God of restoration. But notice how God uses His people to restore other people. God accomplishes the act of restoration through Job. The three musketeers of misery come to Job with sacrifices of repentance and restoration. A true understanding of God's rebuilding means that we are willing to become part of the blueprint for the rebuilding of others. How can I be offered the grace of God and not offer it to someone else?

Once Job accepts the sacrifice of his friends and lifts them up to the Lord, rebuilding begins in his own life. Job 42:10 states, "After Job had prayed for his friends, the LORD made him prosperous again and gave him twice as much as he had before." We see in the following verses that this prosperity included restoration with his own family. The Bible says that "everyone he had known before" came to fellowship with him.

This has to be a powerful moment in Job's journey. Can you even imagine how lonely Job felt after the loss of his children and the abandonment from his wife? Then his closest friends criticize him and stab him with pointed words. But now everyone is gathered around him once again. The cold loneliness has now been replaced with the warmth of close companions. And may I add that the fellowship is so much sweeter when we have experienced full repentance. Instead of spending time with his acquaintances with a chip on his shoulder, he can enjoy the reunion with a grace-filled heart.

Let me offer a couple of observations from this passage. The first observation is that grace holds no grudges. Some of you are crying out for rebuilding. You long for new construction in your life. But you are asking God for grace that you are not willing to give away to others. You will never know full restoration until you let go of all grudges.

Another observation is that God used a broken man to repair others. Job has been broken in all facets of life, but is still useful to God. Job is shattered but God says, "Job, you are valuable to me and you still have a purpose. As I rebuild your life I want to use you for Kingdom purposes. As you have been healed, I want to use you for healing in other people's lives." Some of us have bought into the lie that since you are broken into so many pieces, God could never use you again. In life's dark valleys we can easily lose sight of the greater picture. God loves us and has a wonderful plan for our lives. Let me remind you today that you are valuable to God. You are His child. You have been placed on this earth for a purpose. Pain doesn't void that purpose but completes it.

God took the worst of circumstances in Job's life and made him prosperous again. I don't care what you have been through or what side of the tracks you come from. I don't care how long you have had to sit on a heap of ashes or how messy your life has been. You can be assured that God uses everything for a purpose. God takes every broken piece and makes something beautiful. Have you ever taken a close look at a stained-glass window? These windows are pieces of broken glass made into a stunning masterpiece. God is the master artist turning the broken pieces of your life into a masterpiece. By the way, it takes time to make a masterpiece. You can't rush it. It is a process.

God recovers the pieces

The third part of the rebuilding process is that God recovers the pieces. The rebuilding process will require repentance. Second it will restore relationships. Thirdly it recovers the broken pieces. Please note one key word in Job 42:10. The key word is "after." God recovered the lost pieces in Job's life after he repented and after he forgave his friends. In our selfish mentality, we must be cautious concerning our desires. When we think of the word "prosperous," we often jump immediately to financial gain. But did you notice God's requirements for restoration before He started replacing the missing pieces? God is more concerned with your heart and your relationships than He is with your checking account or padded wallet. The pieces came together AFTER Job repented and AFTER he prayed for his friends.

We should notice both the order of events and the process of rebuilding. We discover in Job 42:11 that the family and friends brought Job a piece of silver and a gold ring. Many commentators say that God is now using the friends and the family who once had abandoned him as a part of the rebuilding journey. It's the seed money to rebuild his livestock and his career. Job has to restart somewhere, but it will take patience to fully recover.

Revealing the heart of God

Fourth, the rebuilding process reveals the heart of God. Remember that the presence of pain does not mean the absence of God. What seems like silence is actually an intentional pause before the page is turned to the next chapter of life. Construction and reconstruction takes time.

During the process we can observe that the heart of God is about relationships. There is an important repetition in the last chapter of Job that we shouldn't miss. Let's take a look at Job 42:7-8:

> After the LORD had said these things to Job, he said to Eliphaz the Temanite, "I am angry with you and your two friends, because you have not spoken of me what is right, as *my servant* Job has. So now take seven bulls and seven rams and go to *my servant* Job and sacrifice a burnt offering for yourselves. *My servant* Job will pray for you, and I will accept his prayer and not deal with you according to your folly. You have not spoken of me what is right, as *my servant* Job has." *(Emphasis mine)*

In only two verses the words "my servant" is repeated four times! Now hang on to these verses and let's take a look back in chapter 1. Job 1:8 says, "Then the Lord said to Satan, 'Have you considered my servant Job?'" Wow! The very first time God mentions the name of Job He describes him as "my servant." The book of Job begins and ends with this title of relationship. Job isn't some impersonal pawn in God's cosmic game of life. To the contrary, Job is God's personal servant.

Even through the pain and turmoil of life, Job has always been God's servant. We could paraphrase: "You know Job? He's MINE. You know, the Job from the land of Uz. He's with Me. He's always been mine and whatever he goes through in life,

HE IS MINE!"

I have great news for you! If you have received Jesus Christ as your Savior then you are a precious child of His. You are God's on the highest mountain and in the darkest valley. Life's troubles don't negate the relationship, they enhance it. Real trust is built when we weather the storms with another. Maybe your current storm is really a blessing moving you to the right shelter, God's shelter. He wants you to know Him better. Enjoy letting the relationship grow in all seasons.

A second way we see the heart of God is through redemption. The final verses, Job 42:16-17, states, "After this, Job lived a hundred and forty years; he saw his children and their children to the fourth generation. And so he died, old and full of years." Job experienced long life and the rewards of watching generations of his own family. By the way, my favorite word in this verse has to be "full." After dozens of chapters of emptiness, the final description of Job's life is "full." God's redemption is complete. God's redemption is fulfilling. God will not leave anything empty in your life.

In the New Testament, it is God's redemption of Job's life that is remembered. There is only one mention of Job in the New Testament. It is found in the book of James. The scripture states in James 5:11 "As you know, we consider blessed those who have persevered. You have heard of Job's perseverance and have seen what the Lord finally brought about. The Lord is full of compassion and mercy." What did the Lord finally bring about after Job persevered? Compassion and mercy!

Our relationship with God happens because of His grace. Our sins are forgiven because of His grace. We survive every day because of His compassion. When this life is over, we will enter heaven based on His grace. Persevere my friend. Life is not about us anyway. We live through His grace. "For it is by grace you have been saved, through faith—and this not from yourselves, it is the gift of God—not by works, so that no one can boast" (Ephesians 2:8-9).

Rebuilding can be tough. It will take time. But it's worth it! Life begins when we establish a personal relationship with God through His Son Jesus Christ. And our patient, grace-filled God doesn't believe in disposable relationships. He isn't going to remove His shelter during the storm. Wait and watch! God is at work and He is not finished with you.

My favorite epitaph is found on the simple stone grave marker of Ruth Graham at the Billy Graham Library in Charlotte, North Carolina. It reads, "End of Construction. Thank you for your patience." The rebuilding process doesn't end until we meet our Savior face-to-face on the other side of eternity. Be patient with God's rebuilding!

CHAPTER TEN

Ultimate Solution for Pain

The title for this chapter may sound too good to be true. Some readers may have skipped ahead to this chapter because an ultimate solution is what most people desire. We live in a culture that tries to sell us anything to relieve pain. In case you don't believe me, just spend a few hours watching the Saturday afternoon infomercials. It seems as if we have found a cure for everything. Does your back hurt? If so, there's a pill or a machine that claims to fix it. Do your feet hurt? For the low payment $19.95, you can have a shoe insert shipped to your house in the next 5 to 7 days. Maybe a headache is your ailment. Then wait no longer—there's a supplement that will help you feel young again. Just a few decades ago, magic elixirs were sold by street vendors. Now a miracle cure is being delivered to our living rooms via the television. The world is telling us that there is a cure for the pain that ails you.

Unfortunately, many of us have garages and medicine cabinets filled with false hope. Those magic products weren't so magic after all. So is there really an ultimate solution for the pain in your life? The truth of the matter is that our pain is much deeper than the physical. You may be living in a personal prison of mental and emotional bondage. The ache in your heart is crying out for help.

Before we can discuss the ultimate solution, we must settle the issue of worldview. Are you looking at life from a temporal perspective or an eternal one? This is a foundational question that must be answered. If you believe that the ultimate answer

93

for hope will happen through the world's temporary gimmicks, you will be repeatedly disappointed. I have watched people spin through the revolving door of earthly solutions to discover they are right back where they started—hopeless and hurting.

Everything I have ever owned has either rotted, rusted, or faded out. Nothing in this world will last. This includes our earthly bodies. The mortality rate has always been and will always be 100%. Modern inventions and human creativity can't stop the reality of death every human must face. The world will always try to slow the symptoms of decline, but nothing can stop the fact that everyone must face what happens after death. What good is a solution for the pain if it doesn't last forever? What the world needs and what God has provided is a solution for pain that is out of this world.

Real hope for the real pain of life is found in John 3:16. "For God so loved the world that he gave his one and only Son, that whoever believes in him shall not perish but have eternal life." God loves you so much that He wants you to have hope forever. This cannot be accomplished with your good works or well-intentioned efforts. Eternal life, the ultimate freedom from pain forever, is found only in Jesus Christ.

We all start out in this world with a problem. The problem is sin. Romans 3:23 says, "For all have sinned and fall short of the glory of God." We are separated from God by our rebellion. The worst pain in life is separation from God. God created you to have a relationship with Him. It hurts when that relationship is broken.

Mankind has tried everything to reach God. You may think that good works, religion, philosophy, or simply a good life will be enough to reach God. Please note the following critical distinction. Religion is man trying to work his way to God. Christianity is God coming to us through His Son Jesus Christ.

God loves you so much that He doesn't want you to live in pain and separation. Romans 5:8 says, "But God demonstrates his own love for us in this: While we were still sinners, Christ died for us."

Our response to this great love will either be to accept it or reject it. Everyone must choose what they will do with Jesus Christ. You can have an eternal relationship with God by accepting His gift of grace. Romans 10:9 says, "That if you confess with your mouth, 'Jesus is Lord,' and believe in your heart that God raised him from the dead, you will be saved."

When you make the decision to trust Christ, you cross over from a life of death and separation to one of peace, forgiveness, abundant and eternal life. Jesus said in John 10:10, "I have come that they may have life, and have it to the full." The decision to trust Christ must come from you and you alone. No one can make the choice for you. To receive Him, you need to admit that you are a sinner, be willing to repent (turn from your sins), and believe that Jesus Christ died for you on the cross, and rose from the grave. If you have never opened your heart to Jesus Christ, you can do it right now by praying the following prayer:

> Dear Jesus,
> I know that I am a sinner and I ask for your
> forgiveness. I believe You died for my sins and
> rose from the dead. I turn from my sins and invite
> You to come into my life. You shed your blood to
> cover my sins and are alive today. I want to trust
> and follow You as my Lord and Savior. In Your
> Name, Amen.

If you prayed that prayer, I want to welcome you to the family of God. You must understand that a life trusting Jesus doesn't mean a pain-free life. Jesus warned, "In this world you will have trouble. But take heart! I have overcome the world" (John 16:33). There's that eternal perspective again. Yes, this fallen world will come with trouble, but we follow the One who has overcome the world.

The ultimate solution for pain goes back to where we started and ended with the life of Job. It's all about the relationship. Having a relationship with God doesn't mean the absence of pain, but it does mean the presence of God. And that's enough! Knowing that God is near changes everything. Many of life's events will shake our core. We will travel in the valleys and on the mountain tops. But what we need is peace. The absolute peace that God is at work when we cannot see the full picture. We need peace that supersedes our thoughts. Philippians 4:7 states, "And the peace of God, which transcends all understanding, will guard your hearts and your minds in Christ Jesus." There is a peace that is higher and greater than your worst pain.

The ultimate solution for your pain is nothing but God Himself. His nearness and peace carries you through. When it seems as if your world is spinning out of control, it's the presence of God that reminds you that He not only created the world, but also holds it firmly in His mighty hand. He will not leave you nor forsake you. That's a promise. This world comes with its share of hard knocks, but God will not allow you to be knocked out. Remember, the victory is His!

In closing, don't forget that His presence is forever when you trust Him as your Savior. He will be with you here on earth and you will be with Him in heaven forever. You are His child. You are precious to Him. He loved Job and He loves you! If you are longing for a place with no more pain, rest assured that it is coming. Heaven is right around the corner. This life will vanish like a vapor, but eternity with God is closer than you think. Revelation 21:4 says, "He will wipe every tear from their eyes. There will be no more death or mourning or crying or pain, for the old order of things has passed away." In that place, we will say goodbye to pain, forever!

New from Auxano Press!

Are you looking for new and refreshing resources for small group Bible study?

Are you frustrated with a curriculum nobody reads?

Does it bother you that most curriculum pieces are thrown away soon after use?

Auxano Press is providing a new kind of small group study that your people will be eager to study and to keep:

- small book curriculum pieces
- non-disposable
- foundation for building a Christian library
- 12- or 13-week study
- audio teacher's commentary
- free teaching helps available online
- Doctrine, Old Testament, New Testament and Bible in Life study available each year

Each study will be designed for 12- or 13-week study based on the preferred calendar of each church. The first (optional) lesson is an overview which is provided for the teacher to preview the material. The books are then distributed and are formatted in 12 small chapters of 1750 to 2000 words. Optional audio teacher's commentary by the author will be available on two CDs or by download for MP3 player. All other teaching helps are provided online for free from **auxanopress.com**.

Each year **Auxano Press** will provide a doctrine study, an Old Testament book study, A New Testament book study, and a Bible in Life study. Three studies are currently available. *Core Convictions* explores the basics of evangelical theology. The doctrine of the church is the focus of *Connected Community*. *Live It Up* is a topical (Bible in Life) study that will challenge your people to live with missional focus.

Introduction to the Old Testament (Ken Hemphill) and *Introduction to the New Testament* (Kie Bowman) will be out early 2012.

Look for other books by authors such as Danny Akin, Kie Bowman, Rick Byargeon, John Cross, Steve Gaines, Trey Oswald, Ryan Pack, Danny Sinquefield, Eric Thomas, Heath Thomas, David Wheeler and Don Wilton.

WHERE DO i BELONG?

Can a person be a fully COMMITTED follower of Christ and not LOVE His bride, THE CHURCH?

This small book, *Connected Community: Becoming Family through Church*, explores the mystery of God's eternal plan to reveal His manifold wisdom through His church.

FREE STUDY GUIDES for 7- or 13-week study are available at AuxanoPress.com

These products are available by visiting www.lifeway.com or by visiting your local LifeWay Christian Store. Also available at www.auxanopress.com.